ZITA STEYN

Good
Better
Green

The most inventive recipes
to help you eat more greens

Photography by Nassima Rothacker

quadrille

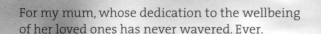

For my mum, whose dedication to the wellbeing
of her loved ones has never wavered. Ever.

Recipe notes

When budget, availability and time allow, I recommend
the following:

- organic meat, dairy products, gelatine and eggs from humanely
  treated animals that have been pastured and allowed to roam free
- good-quality stock, preferably homemade
- sustainable seafood from unpolluted waters
- raw (or unpasteurised) cider vinegar, dairy products, coconut
  oil and water, and honey
- extra virgin olive oil and other good-quality cold-pressed oils
- organic or minimally sprayed fresh local and seasonal produce,
  preferably biodynamically grown
- organic unwaxed citrus fruits, especially if zesting
- organic and preservative-free ingredients, such as condiments,
  sausages, wine, coconut milk and dried fruit (sweetened with
  fruit juice, if at all)
- filtered water, especially when used for fermenting or preserving
- soaking (and even sprouting) grains, nuts, seeds and legumes
  before cooking and/or consuming

Contents

Introduction

My approach to food has been largely shaped by my upbringing in an active, unfussy and lively household. My mother had always taken her responsibility of feeding us, her four boisterous children, extremely seriously, and although I was slightly embarrassed at the time, I still recall the feeling of awe every time I opened a lunch box she had prepared. When I was at primary school, my mum fell ill with chronic fatigue syndrome for several years, and only managed to claw her way out of the black hole by implementing a complete overhaul of her – and our! – lifestyle. It meant studying nutrition and holistic medicine in great depth, drastically reducing sugar and refined foods even more, and preparing meals that withstood the rigorous test of being whole, wholesome and health-supportive. But amazingly the food still tasted fantastic!

This book was born out of the one question that almost all my clients and friends have asked me at some point: "How do I incorporate more green vegetables into my diet?" That was all the inspiration I needed to create this collection of honest, delicious and interesting dishes based on a real need by real people.

Green vegetables, in particular the dark-green leafy kind, are the most nutrient-dense foods available to us. They contain an array of potent compounds that are very difficult to find anywhere else in the same concentration. Green vegetables are rich in dietary fibre, folic acid, beta-carotene, vitamin C, vitamin K, potassium and magnesium, as well as containing a host of phytochemicals that can reduce inflammation and eliminate carcinogens. They contain a variety of carotenoids, flavonoids and other powerful antioxidants that prohibit the oxidation of molecules in the body and are thought to prevent several degenerative diseases. Some green vegetables are also a major source of iron and calcium. In addition to these, sea vegetables (many of them a dark green-black), contain all of the 56 elements essential for human health in bio-available form, together with important trace elements like selenium that are often lacking in land vegetables due to soil demineralisation.

Over 2,000 years ago, Hippocrates said that all illness begins in the gut. And today many experts still believe there is a lot of truth in that. How can we expect to power our hard-working engines if we don't prioritise the fuel we put into them? Some of the recipes in this book may use a few more ingredients and seem a little more time-consuming than you are used to, but they are certainly not difficult to make and they are well worth the effort. Anyone can put something on a plate and call it supper, but only those who know how to combine flavours and use all the varied aromatics nature has to offer, will serve up a meal that is not only medicine for the body, but also food for the soul.

Zita

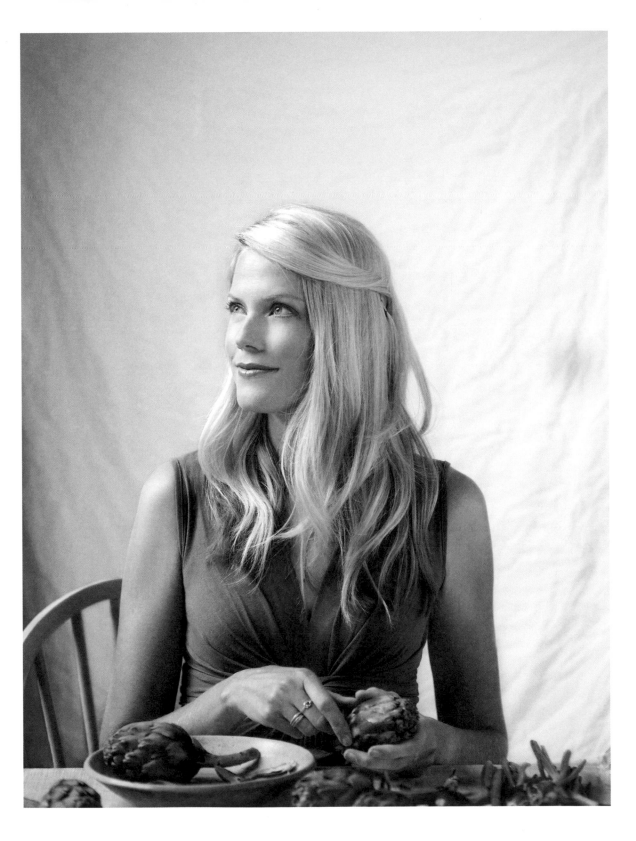

Green champions

It is wonderful to see how the tide is turning and that ever more people are becoming aware of the crucial role that good, nutritious food plays in a healthy life. Most of us now know that eating lots of vegetables, especially green ones, is vital. One question I often get asked, however, is how to incorporate these green vegetables on a daily basis. And so the idea for this book was born. In it you will find suggestions on how to use many different kinds of green vegetables, with a particular focus on leafy greens. Feel free to substitute and experiment – once you are familiar with these wonderful foods, you will no doubt find many more ways to enjoy them!

A word of advice: try not to get stuck on a few trusty friends. It is important to rotate between all the different vegetables, because each belongs to a different family that boasts a unique nutritional profile. Dark-green leafy vegetables are high in calcium and iron, and the bioavailability of the calcium is actually higher in kale and other dark-green leafy vegetables (like broccoli) than in dairy, but you need to eat a large variety of calcium-containing plant foods to ensure you are getting enough. Many vegetables also contain small amounts of toxins as a defence mechanism to protect the plant against predators. If consumed in excess these toxins could have a negative impact on your health, for example, the goitrogens in cruciferous vegetables could interfere with thyroid hormone function in susceptible individuals, and the oxalic acid in – amongst others – spinach, chard and beet(root) greens may inhibit mineral absorption and lead to kidney stone formation in those prone. Rotating between them will therefore ensure you gain the maximum advantage of all the wonderful nutrients they have to offer, without building up harmful levels of any toxin.

Aquatic greens

These are greens that live and grow in or near water. If they are not yet a regular part of your diet, consider finding ways to include them often. Remember to source aquatic greens from clean waters.

SEAWEEDS

Green sea vegetables are extremely nutritious, as they offer one of the broadest ranges of minerals of any food, containing almost all the minerals found in the ocean, including iodine, copper, iron, zinc, potassium, phosphorus and manganese. They contain a variety of unique phytonutrients, including the potent fucoidans, that appear to have anti-tumour, anti-cancer and neuro-protective actions. Unlike some other categories of vegetables, sea vegetables do not appear to depend on carotenoids and flavonoids for their antioxidant benefits because they contain several other types, including alkaloid antioxidants. Sea vegetables are also an excellent source of vitamins A, C, thiamin, riboflavin, niacin and B6.

WATERCRESS

Spidery watercress – well known to many as a garnish and almost always pushed to one side by diners – is not only one of the most nutrient-dense foods available to us, but its peppery leaves are also very exciting to eat and cook with. Although this plant is technically a member of the brassica family (see page 10) and botanically related to garden cress, rocket and mustard, I have included it in this group, as it is considered an aquatic or semi-aquatic perennial plant that is often found near slow-moving water. Amongst the oldest-known leafy greens consumed by humans, watercress contains significant amounts of iron, calcium, iodine and folic acid, as well as vitamins A and C. It is great in salads and soups, tossed with pasta, on sandwiches, and paired with citrus or seafood, especially smoked fish. The best way to buy and store watercress is in lush bunches and in a small jug of water.

SAMPHIRE

A distinction is made between rock samphire, found on cliffs or in rocks and shingle on the Mediterranean coast, and marsh samphire (also known as sea beans, sea asparagus or glasswort), a succulent that also grows near the sea, but prefers estuaries and wetlands rich in minerals and trace elements. Samphire is a good diuretic, believed to aid digestion, and is rich in vitamin C. Choose stalks that are bright green and firm, wash them well and use as soon as possible. They only need a minute or two of steaming or stir-frying, but can be enjoyed raw too. Remember not to add any salt to the dish, as samphire is very salty.

SIMPLE WAYS TO EAT AQUATIC GREENS:

1. Combine *watercress* with other lettuces in a salad with sliced oranges and avocados, and serve with a simple vinaigrette.

2. Sprinkle a pinch of dried *kelp* flakes into soups or stews while cooking.

3. Make a side dish with quinoa, finely chopped herbs and *watercress*, chopped tomatoes and finely chopped onions. Add lemon juice, olive oil and salt.

4. Rinse *arame* and soak for 5 minutes, before adding to sautéing vegetables such as carrots, slow-cooked onions, winter squash, lotus root and some shiitake mushrooms.

5. Sauté garlic and *samphire* for a minute, then add slivers of lightly steamed asparagus. Serve with a drizzle of olive oil.

6. Chop and simmer together a bunch of *watercress*, a couple of pears, garlic, onions, a potato or two and some ginger in a pot with stock, then blend until smooth for a revitalising soup.

7. Chopped, rehydrated *hijiki* and *arame* are delicious added to cooked rice, millet or barley.

8. Make a *watercress* sauce for grilled fish by mixing finely chopped watercress, lemon juice, crème fraîche or thick natural yogurt and sea salt.

9. Toast *nori* sheets in a hot pan and eat as a snack.

10. Finely chop *samphire* and add to a kedgeree a minute before serving.

Green brassica (or cruciferous) vegetables

Pungent, potent brassicas – all members of the mustard family – are the undisputed heavy-hitters in the vegetable world. Not only is almost every part (root, stalk, stem, leaf, bud, flower, sprout and seed) of a plant used for food in this family, they are also rich in vitamins, minerals and antioxidants, and contain very high levels of phytochemicals, the non-nutritive substances in plants that have been shown to fight carcinogens, inflammation and liver toxicity, and generally support good health. Most brassicas improve taste-wise, and become less pungent and more digestible, with gentle cooking, such as steaming, or a brief sauté.

KALE, CURLY KALE AND CAVOLO NERO

In addition to providing high levels of vitamins and flavonoids, superheroes kale & co contain several natural components (called glucosinolates) that are converted into sulphur-containing phytochemicals (called isothiocyanates) in the digestive tract, and these in turn are thought to help prevent several types of cancer and, in some cases, even suppress the growth of cancerous tumours. Thanks to their broad nutritional profile, these vegetables are also believed to help fight cardiovascular disease, asthma, rheumatoid arthritis and premature ageing of the skin, and to promote the health of the urinary tract. Finally, all common kale cultivars provide plenty of carotenoids which, amongst others, are known for their ability to support eye health. Cavolo nero is called black cabbage Tuscan kale, dinosaur kale or lacinato.

SPRING GREENS AND COLLARDS

These spring cabbages are similar to kale in that the central leaves only form a very loose head, thus giving us silky, easy-to-prepare leaves without the crunch of round cabbages. Being loose, all the leaves are fully exposed to light, and so more strongly flavoured, but are also particularly rich in vitamin C, folic acid and dietary fibre. They are considered to be closer to wild cabbage than most other domesticated forms.

ROCKET AND MUSTARD GREENS

Rocket is an annual herb that varies from mild in flavour and similar to baby spinach in appearance when young, to peppery, bitter and with elongated lobular leaves when mature. Mustard greens (also called Indian or Chinese mustard, and leaf mustard) are the greens of a subspecies of the mustard plant and also very peppery, although cooking does reduce this. Like most other dark leafy greens, rocket and mustard greens are a great source of vitamins A, B-complex, C and K, as well as folates.

GREEN CABBAGES AND BRUSSELS SPROUTS

Common green (and red) cabbages, one of the oldest of the brassica vegetables, and the ancestors of broccoli and cauliflower, have thick leaves and round, tightly-wrapped heads. Savoy cabbage has a milder flavour and thinner, more textured leaves. Brussels sprouts look like tiny cabbages, but are in fact buds that form all along tall stalks of the parent plant. Cabbages, like other brassicas, are high in sulphur and rich in phytonutrients antioxidants.

BROCCOLI

Broccoli (regular, tenderstem and broccoli rabe or rapini) contains one of the most powerful phytochemicals – sulforaphane – which is formed when the vegetable is cut, chopped and/or chewed. Bacteria in your intestines can also act on broccoli to produce sulforaphane. This phytochemical is so potent that scientists are interested in developing it as a potential treatment for cancer and autism. Unfortunately frozen broccoli lacks the ability to produce sulforaphane, but researchers are working on a solution, for example adding a small amount of radish powder to the frozen veg.

ASIAN BRASSICAS (PAK CHOY, CHINESE BROCCOLI, TATSOI, NAPA CABBAGE AND MIZUNA)

These are similar in some ways to the more familiar European brassicas, but are faster growing, often more productive and have many and varied uses. Most parts are eaten, used in stir-fries or steamed, but they can also be used as salad greens. Flavours vary from mild to peppery, but they are generally not as pungent or bitter as the other brassicas. Napa cabbage, also called Chinese or celery cabbage, has a more delicate texture and flavour than common cabbage.

ROOT BRASSICAS (KOHLRABI AND WASABI)

The name "kohlrabi" is an amalgamation of the German word for cabbage and the Swiss German word for turnip – and this is a good description of the taste you can expect. I love it raw, either finely chopped, grated or as carpaccio, but it can also be sautéed, roasted or added to stir-fries and stews. The greens are also delicious raw (when young and tender) or wilted.

Wasabi is commonly known as Japanese horseradish, although it is not from a species of horseradish, but rather a brassica. Although wasabi does have a strong, spicy taste, it is different from the taste of chilli peppers, which get their heat from capsaicin that causes a "burning" sensation on the tongue. Wasabi releases chemical vapours that affect the nasal passage. The powerful smell and taste are derived from the high levels of isothiocyanate, the sulphur-containing phytochemical which is believed to combat cancer.

SIMPLE WAYS TO EAT GREEN BRASSICAS:

1. Serve sautéed or steamed *broccoli* or other brassicas with blank canvas foods, such as cooked legumes or rice, and lots of olive oil.

2. Any kind of fat can be used to subdue the flavour of an ingredient, as well as add richness and a wonderful mouth-feel to any dish. Try adding coconut cream to a *kale* and chicken curry, for example, or mixing some nuts and avocado into your dressed *mustard green* and *lettuce* salad.

3. Brassicas are delicious with a variety of chillies or cayenne pepper, and one of my favourite ways with *pak choy* is to sauté it with some salt, garlic and chopped chillies in a little oil, then to toss it with cooked soba noodles. Serve this with virgin sesame oil and sesame seeds.

4. Adding creamy organic (preferably pastured and unpasteurised) dairy products, such as soft cheese, cream or yogurt, to a *brassica* stir-fry or soup, or a dressing intended for a *rocket* salad, makes all the difference.

5. Bold flavours do well alongside salty ingredients, such as olives, hard cheeses, anchovies, smoked or cured meats and fish, capers and shoyu. Try grating some Parmesan over an oven-roasted tray of *Brussels sprouts*.

6. I love the taste of *cabbage* with fruit – raw cabbage with fresh fruit such as an apple and shaven cabbage salad, or sautéed cabbage with dried fruits such as raisins or currants.

7. Try shredding some *spring greens* and frying in a little oil before tossing in a tangy lemon and honey vinaigrette. Adding something sweet to pungent foods often helps balance the flavour.

The beetroot family

Spinach, chard and all the beet cultivars belong to the Amaranth (or Amaranthaceae) family, which is mostly native to tropical America and Africa. This flowering plant family is dominated by herbs but also includes vines, shrubs and trees. Leaves are mostly simple and entire, and flowers regular, cyclic and tiny.

SPINACH

Believed to have originated in Persia, spinach spread across Europe by the 12th century and was desirable for its healthful properties even in those days. Generally you will find two or three different types of spinach: Savoy, with dark-green wrinkled leaves, semi-Savoy, and a flat-leaf type with smooth leaves. Fresh leaves are a rich source of antioxidants, vitamins A and C, flavonoids and carotenoids, which together help protect against free radicals. This green leafy vegetable and its family members also contain good amounts of many B-complex vitamins and vitamin K, as well as being a good source of potassium, manganese, magnesium, copper, zinc and iron. One thing to note with this group of vegetables is the concentration of oxalic acid (especially in more mature plants), which is present but much lower in many other vegetables and plant-based foods, but high enough in this family to interfere with the absorption of minerals such as calcium and iron. To avoid this, rotate your greens, mix high-oxalate greens with lower-oxalate greens, cook the greens and discard the cooking water, or ferment them. On top of that, iron from plant sources (called non-heme iron) as compared to animal sources (heme iron) is quite difficult for your body to absorb, so add some vitamin C-rich foods such as peppers and citrus, or some heme-iron foods to your meal to increase the iron absorption, and avoid foods that may inhibit iron absorption, such as calcium-rich foods, caffeine, cocoa, phytate-rich foods (such as soy, some nuts and seeds, and some legumes), and eggs.

SWISS OR RAINBOW CHARD

Chard (also known as Swiss chard, leaf beet, silver beet, spinach beet, seakale beet, crab beet, mangold, and even just spinach in some countries) is a leafy green vegetable with large leaves that taste a little like spinach, but are slightly sweeter. Younger leaves can be eaten raw in salads, but the fleshy stalks and tougher leaves of more mature plants are usually cooked. Like spinach, chard is full of phytonutrients, vitamins and minerals, and should be briefly boiled or sautéed to retain as many of these as possible. The leaf can be green or reddish and the stalks also vary in colour – usually white, yellow, or red (which is what "rainbow chard" refers to).

SIMPLE WAYS TO EAT THE BEETROOT FAMILY:

1. When making gnocchi from scratch, add some puréed *spinach* and grated nutmeg to the dough.

2. Finely shred *beetroot greens* and add to a beetroot and chickpea curry a few minutes before serving.

3. Add a handful of *spinach* leaves and some sautéed onion to two beaten eggs for an easy breakfast scramble.

4. Juice younger *beetroot greens* together with lower oxalate lettuces and add a lemon to increase iron absorption.

5. Make a version of the Punjabi potato and *spinach* dish, aloo-palak, by sautéing a bay leaf, pinch of ground cloves, and some ground cinnamon and turmeric until fragrant, then adding chopped onions, garlic paste and grated ginger, and cooking this with chopped tomatoes until soft. Stir in finely chopped, cooked spinach and cubed cooked potatoes, and season to taste.

6. Cook the stems and leaves of *rainbow chard* until tender, then finely shred and stir into lightly steamed carrots and peas with a knob of salted butter.

7. Top crispy rye toast with sautéed *beetroot greens*, soft goat's cheese, fresh figs and a drizzle of aged balsamic vinegar.

8. Use briefly blanched large-leaf *spinach* or *chard* leaves to make parcels filled with cooked lentils, onion, chopped fresh herbs, grated ginger and spices, such as paprika and allspice.

9. *Swiss chard*, caramelised onions and goat's cheese are great together in a tart or quiche.

The daisy family

The Asteraceae or Compositae (commonly known as the aster, daisy or sunflower family) are a large family of flowering plants with over 23,600 species and 13 subfamilies. Many members have composite flowers in the form of flower heads, like the star form of its most prominent member, the aster. This family provides us with valuable products such as cooking oils, lettuces, sunflower seeds, artichokes, sweetening agents, coffee substitutes and herbal teas and medicines.

LETTUCES, LEAVES AND BITTER GREENS

Many edible lettuces and leaves fall in the daisy family, including curly endive (or frisée), romaine, cos, chicory or Belgian endive, escarole, radicchio, oak leaf, dandelion, butter (Bibb and Boston) lettuce, iceberg, and loose-leaf lettuce. The leaves all boast different shapes, sizes, colours, textures and tastes. Generally the darker green the leaf, the more nutritious, but they are all a wonderful addition to your diet, being rich in chlorophyll, antioxidants, vitamins and minerals (specifically potassium, calcium, phosphorous, iron and magnesium), and very low in oxalic acid.

Lettuces range in bitterness from mild (such as butter lettuce) to severe (like dandelion or chicory), but don't be put off by it. Like many other green vegetables already discussed, the bitterness in edible leaves triggers a chemical reaction in our bodies that has numerous health benefits, such as helping to absorb nutrients by stimulating the production of gastric acid, enzyme production and bile flow. Bitter foods also help balance taste buds, control food cravings and help sweep waste through the digestive tract with the help of fibre and sulphur-based compounds which support the natural detoxification pathways in the liver. Finally, bitter foods and herbs have been shown to boost metabolism, inhibit fat absorption, and prevent insulin spikes.

SIMPLE WAYS TO EAT THE DAISY FAMILY:

1. Toss wilted *escarole lettuce* in harissa paste and serve alongside roast chicken or grilled fish.

2. Prepare *chicory* leaf cups with chopped walnuts and crumbled blue cheese to serve with an apéritif before dinner.

3. Marinade thinly sliced courgette in olive oil, lemon juice and chopped herbs for several hours, then arrange on a platter and garnish with bits of dressed *frisée*, pickled red onions and lemon zest.

4. For a barbecue, cut small heads of *butter lettuce* in half, brush with oil and grill for 2–3 minutes before drizzling with a crème fraîche, chive and lemon dressing.

5. Heat some oil in a pan, add cooked beans (such as cannellini) and fry until crispy before adding some garlic, *dandelion leaves* and salt. As soon as the greens have wilted, drizzle with extra virgin olive oil and serve.

6. Mix different leaves such as loose-leaf, baby *cos* and *radicchio*, and dress with a shallot vinaigrette to serve alongside a rich meal.

7. Roughly chop *romaine lettuce* and toss with chunks of apple, pecan nuts and a tangy yogurt dressing, for a refreshing autumnal salad.

8. Cut *romaine lettuces* in half and spread salsa verde over the surface before roasting in a medium-hot oven for about 10 minutes, until the lettuce is slightly browned around the edges.

9. Toss *curly endive* with hot, roasted squash, finely chopped chives, olive oil, apple cider vinegar and raisins, for a delicious side dish.

10. Cut heads of *chicory* in half, drizzle with oil, season with salt and pepper, and roast in a hot oven for 15 minutes, then top with orange slices and soft goat's cheese, before returning to the oven for another 15–20 minutes, or until tender and golden.

Herbs

What would our culinary world be like without these fragrant plants?! I rely heavily on these green leaves and stems to flavour food, but I also cherish herbs for their medicinal value and even to enliven wardrobes and linens. Traditionally, different regions use specific varieties of herbs, and so a particular combination of flavours will frequently elicit memories of a country once visited or an exotic meal enjoyed. The leaves of many herbs can be dried and used as a substitute for fresh, but they often lose some intensity and create a more earthy flavour rather than provide a hit of freshness. Here are a few more commonly known culinary herbs and ideas for how to use them:

BASIL
A versatile and popular aromatic herb, basil is most often used in Mediterranean and Asian dishes, such as the classic pesto Genovese (made with basil, pine nuts, Parmesan or Pecorino cheese, and olive oil), or a Thai curry made with holy basil (tulsi). If you are a keen gardener, try growing some varieties with interesting flavours, such as pineapple, lemon, clove and anise.

BAY LEAVES
I usually have a large bag of bay leaves at the ready to add whenever I cook grains, legumes or large batches of stocks, soups, sauces and stews. The bittersweet and mildly spicy leaves are best used when cooking times are slightly longer and, together with parsley and thyme, it forms part of the *bouquet garni* added to many classic French recipes. It is one of the few herbs that is equally good fresh or dried.

CHIVES
Chives are top greens in the allium family, which also includes garlic, spring onions (the top greens of immature onions) and leeks. The long, thin and hollow green blades have a mild, grassy flavour and combine perfectly with chervil, parsley and tarragon in the classic French blend known as *fines herbes*. Allium vegetables have been cultivated for centuries, not only for their invaluable pungent flavour, but also for their health benefits. Just like other allium members, chives possess thiosulfinate antioxidants, which convert to allicin – an organosulfur compound – by enzymatic reaction when its leaves are cut, chopped or crushed. Studies have found that allicin, which has anti-bacterial, anti-viral, and anti-fungal properties, is most potent directly after the cell membranes have been disturbed, and that heat destroys it. Allicin has also been found to help reduce cholesterol production, blood pressure and overall risk of coronary artery disease, peripheral vascular diseases and stroke.

CORIANDER

Coriander (cilantro) is the only herb I know of that elicits a "love or hate" response, but it is nonetheless used commonly across the world. Its tender stems and vibrant green leaves, not dissimilar in appearance to flat-leaf parsley, have a fresh, citrus taste, and very strong aroma. Leaf coriander is best added to a dish just before serving, but coriander seeds (the dried berries) can withstand heat and longer cooking times. Coriander is very rich in phytonutrients and antioxidants. Its leaves and seeds contain various essential oils and the plant is considered to be an antiseptic, analgesic, aphrodisiac, digestive aid, fungicide and natural stimulant. It is also a very good source of vitamins A, C, K and traces of the B vitamins, and calcium, potassium, iron, manganese and sodium.

DILL

This green herb, with its wiry, thread-like leaves, has been used for culinary and medicinal purposes for hundreds of years. Like coriander, the seeds can also be used. Dill's distinctive, slightly bitter taste is a combination of anise (or liquorice), fennel and celery. Dill's unique medicinal value is ascribed to mainly two healing components, namely monoterpenes – phytonutrients that exhibit an aromatic ring – and flavonoids, but it is also rich in minerals and certain amino acids. The health benefits of dill include its ability to boost digestive health, as well as provide relief from insomnia, hiccups, diarrhoea, dysentery, menstrual disorders, respiratory disorders and cancer. It is also good for oral care, can be a powerful boost for the immune system and can protect from bone degradation. It is also an anti-inflammatory substance, so it can protect against arthritis, and relieve flatulence.

MARJORAM

Sweet marjoram – valued for centuries for its culinary and medicinal uses – is one of the most popular herbs used throughout the Mediterranean region. It is delicate and slightly sweet-tasting with a subtle pungency. In the US it is often referred to as, and confused with its bolder cousin, oregano. Marjoram is very effective in the treatment of coughs and colds. It is considered a potent decongestant and helps fight viral infection, bronchitis, sinusitis and sinus headaches. It is also believed to have a calming effect and support cardiac health due to its flavonoid content, and is a wonderful aid in digestion-related disorders.

MINT

The herb often associated with a fresh breath is also a very versatile kitchen companion. Of the two dozen species, the one grown and used most widely is spearmint, but peppermint, with its darker green leaves and sharper flavour, is also used, mainly to flavour confectionery and ice cream. Mint has antiseptic qualities, aids digestion (by activating the salivary and digestive enzyme glands), and is known to soothe respiratory complaints. I particularly like mint for its ability to naturally uplift and stimulate when I am having a low point.

OREGANO (OR WILD MARJORAM)

I have used oregano several times in the recipes in this book, as it is really delicious and has some wonderful health benefits. Origanum bushes produce strong stems with dark-green leaves that have a pungent, slightly floral and bitter taste with citrus undertones. This herb loves garlic and lamb, and can hold its own when combined with vinegar or lemon. Like most herbs, oregano has a much higher antioxidant level than other fruit and vegetables, and is also rich in vitamins and minerals. Additionally, oregano contains potent antimicrobial phytochemicals, and has some anti-viral properties.

PARSLEY

This is my favourite multi-tasker. Even though it has a distinct flavour, it is strangely neutral and manages to blend in with many foods and flavours. I often toss a handful into my smoothie and whenever I feel a meal lacks chlorophyll, I add a huge amount of finely chopped parsley. There are two main varieties: curly-leaf and flat-leaf, with the latter having a slightly stronger taste. Parsley belongs to the *Apiaceae* family, along with carrots, celery, and other herbs like cumin, dill, lovage, angelica, and anise. The herb contains valuable volatile oils and flavonoids that have chemo-protective benefits and act as antioxidants to protect cells from oxidative damage and stress. The herb is also anti-bacterial, anti-inflammatory, and a great source of vitamin C and beta-carotene (pro-vitamin A).

ROSEMARY

We have a huge rosemary bush in our garden and I run out for twigs regularly throughout the year. The pine needle-like leaves are a versatile flavouring agent that can be used in a vast number of dishes. Add the whole stem to a pot roast or strip the leaves off and chop them up very finely before including in a wintry pasta dish. Rosemary has also been used as a natural remedy for a variety of ailments over the centuries. It has powerful antioxidant, anti-inflammatory, antibacterial and anti-carcinogenic properties, is said to improve memory, lift mood, relieve migraines and pain in general, detoxify the liver, and help treat digestive problems. It can also be used as a natural remedy for respiratory problems.

SAGE

Native to the Mediterranean and Balkans, sage is a member of the mint family and has a very strong, musty, slightly bitter flavour, so use with care. Sage leaves are greyish-green (sometimes purple) and velvety, and can withstand long cooking times. In fact, sage is very rarely eaten raw. Often used with poultry, sage seems to go especially well with fatty dishes and is believed to aid in their digestion. Its antiseptic and astringent properties make sage ideal for many conditions of the mouth and throat, and it is also said to improve memory.

TARRAGON

Often used in French cooking (it is one of the herbs that makes up *fines herbes* and is used in Béarnaise sauce), this herb has long, soft, bright-green leaves and an aniseed flavour with a hint of vanilla. A perfect match for poultry, fish, eggs and cheese, use fresh or dried tarragon to flavour dishes, sauces, or condiments. This herb has been used by numerous cultures for centuries as a natural treatment for many ailments (such as toothache and digestive issues), and is high in vitamins, potassium and other nutrients that have been proven to provide health benefits.

THYME

Another member of the mint family, subtle thyme (in all its varieties) is an essential component of any cook's arsenal. It grows in long, thin sprigs with small green leaves, which are mostly stripped from the stalk, although whole sprigs can also be added to dishes such as stews, soups and sauces, and removed before serving. It pairs well with other Mediterranean herbs like oregano and marjoram, and is used throughout Italian, French and Mediterranean cooking. Just like the other herbs, thyme is packed with health-promoting components. Amongst others it supports eye health, helps cure coughs and colds, has antibacterial properties, helps control blood pressure, improves bone health and aids digestion.

SIMPLE WAYS TO EAT HERBS:

1. Toast fresh *oregano* leaves lightly in a pan before adding them to your favourite chilli con carne recipe.

2. Sprinkle fresh whole leaves of *marjoram* in a salad of greens.

3. Put fresh *tarragon* sprigs and peeled garlic cloves into a sterilised bottle with cider vinegar. Place in a dark spot for a few days and remove the sprigs once the desired strength has been reached.

4. Wrap several *rosemary* twigs in some muslin and add to a pot of beans while they are cooking. You will impart the flavour without having to pick out hundreds of needles.

5. Scatter *oregano* leaves over cubes of goat's milk feta and mixed olives, then drizzle with olive oil.

6. Finely shred fresh *mint* and add to chocolate chip cookie dough.

7. Toss *marjoram* and toasted pecans with thinly sliced oranges and leeks dressed with pecan oil.

8. Add fresh *thyme* leaves to a marinade for vegetable kebabs at your next barbecue.

9. One of the best uses for *oregano* in your cooking is adding it to a dry rub or a marinade for meat (that includes cloves, cinnamon, rosemary, ginger, black pepper, paprika, garlic) prior to cooking, which may help reduce the toxic compounds created during the cooking process.

10. For a great snack, place a fresh anchovy between two *sage* leaves and fry in some hot oil until crisp.

Liquid greens

Juices/smoothies

- Aim to use more vegetables than fruit when preparing fresh juices. Make this shift gradually if you are new to juicing.

- Freshly pressed vegetable juices are a useful way of increasing nutrient intake, especially in those with digestive problems or other health issues.

- Freshly juiced tonics should be consumed as soon as possible after making, as exposure to light and oxygen starts degrading the juice at once.

- Buy produce that's been minimally sprayed with pesticides, as you are using the whole fruit or veg.

- Vegetable juices should be seen as a nutrient supplement under normal circumstances and not as a meal replacement unless you are following a juice-based detox for a few days. Smoothies, on the other hand, are akin to a (liquid) meal, so bear this in mind when you have a large smoothie and feel entitled to a fry-up, too!

- To increase nutrient absorption:
  1. Drink green juices on an empty stomach or two hours after having eaten, and wait at least 20 minutes before eating your next meal
  2. Consume some fat with juices and smoothies (liquid coconut oil, nuts or nut butters and seeds)
  3. Drink juices and smoothies at room temperature – it is kinder on your digestion
  4. Always include a vitamin C-rich food (such as lemon or lime) in your green juice and smoothie, or have some soon after, as this helps reduce the effect of the oxalic acid or anti-nutrients found in many leafy greens (such as spinach and chard)

- Alternate greens frequently. Regular consumption of raw cruciferous vegetables, for example, may affect those with thyroid dysfunction due to the goitrogens.

- Always start juicing with the leafy greens and herbs, followed by the soft fruits and ginger, and lastly any chunky produce such as apple, carrot, celery or cucumber, to help the juicer do its job.

- Chew your drinks and drink your food! If you don't swirl the drink around in your mouth and chew a few times, the digestive process, which starts with saliva production in the mouth and a signal being sent to the brain to release digestive juices in the stomach, is compromised.

Juices
ALL SERVE 2–3

1. Citrus green

Very refreshing and just like a cold citron pressé, only bright green.

200g kale (stalks and leaves)

Small handful of parsley

1 cucumber

1 lemon, partially peeled (leave about one-fifth of the skin on)

1 lime, peeled

2 green apples (or red ones for a sweeter taste)

Wash all the ingredients well and chop into manageable chunks, then juice in the order listed. Stir and serve.

2. Lettuce and pear

200g cos or other crunchy leaf lettuce

Large handful of basil leaves

2 ripe pears

1 lime, partially peeled (leave about half the skin on)

1 satsuma, mandarin or tangerine, peeled

Wash all the ingredients well and chop into manageable chunks, then juice in the order listed. You may want to pass the juice through a sieve to filter out any soft pulp that might have slipped through. Otherwise, it will be a little thicker than a regular juice. Stir and serve.

3. Spring greens, pineapple and ginger

I love the spiciness the cabbage greens add to this juice, but it might not be the easiest way to get your family drinking green juices, so feel free to replace the spring greens with other greens of your choice.

150g spring greens, collards or green cabbage, tough stalks removed, roughly chopped

½ cucumber

1 orange, partially peeled (leave about one fifth of the skin on)

½ ripe pineapple, peeled

Knob of ginger (large if you like it spicy)

½ lemon, peeled

Wash all the ingredients well and chop into manageable chunks, then juice in the order listed. Stir and serve.

4. Lamb's lettuce, green grape and kiwi

200g lamb's lettuce (mâche) or baby spinach leaves

Large handful of mint leaves

150g green grapes

3 kiwi fruit, unpeeled

½ cucumber

1 celery stalk

Wash all the ingredients well and chop into manageable chunks, then juice in the order listed.

Either give the juice a quick whizz in a blender for an ultra-smooth, thick juice, or pass it through a sieve to filter out any soft pulp that may have slipped through. Stir and serve.

Nettle and dandelion infusion

Both nettle tips and dandelion leaves are renowned for their medicinal properties and should be available in select healthfood stores or ethnic grocers. I always have different infusion blends on the shelf to offer my guests, be it for their relaxing, immune-boosting or energising properties.
MAKES ENOUGH FOR ROUGHLY 15 CUPS OF TEA

15g dried nettle leaves

15g dried dandelion leaves

10g dried peppermint leaves

2 tablespoons fennel seeds, crushed with pestle and mortar or partially ground in a spice grinder

5g dried red rose petals

Mix all the ingredients together well and store in an airtight container.

To make a single serving of the infusion, put 1 heaped tablespoon of the loose leaf tea in a teapot and pour 250–300ml boiling water over. Allow to steep for 2–3 minutes, then pour through a strainer to enjoy.

ALL JUICES PHOTOGRAPHED ON PAGES 22–23

Left to right: Spring greens, pineapple and ginger juice; Citrus green juice; Lettuce and pear juice; Lamb's lettuce, green grape and kiwi juice

Smoothies
ALL SERVE 2–3

1. The Pick-me-up

This is a good choice when you need rehydration and energy. Rooibos (redbush) tea, dried figs, blueberries and chia seeds are all rich in antioxidants, and figs contain more fibre than any other fruit. Lamb's lettuce is packed with Vitamin B9, known for its anti-fatigue and anti-stress properties. It is also very rich in eye-protecting Vitamin A and multitasking Vitamin B6. To top it off, it has almost as high an iron content as spinach, but is very low in oxalates, which prevent nutrients from being absorbed.

250ml strong rooibos tea, cooled

1 teaspoon chia seeds

2 large dried figs, roughly chopped

1 large very ripe banana, cut or broken into chunks

½ teaspoon good-quality vanilla extract

Large handful (about 30g) of lamb's lettuce (mâche)

150g frozen (or fresh) blueberries

Juice of 1 lime

Prepare the tea the night before.

Pour the cooled tea into the blender and add the chia seeds. Stir a few times while you get the rest of your ingredients together.

Now add everything else, including the blueberries, and blend until smooth.

2. Ultimate green

If you are not one for green smoothies in general, you should try this one. It is quite delicious and very virtuous. It helps having a high-speed blender, but if you don't, just keep blending until the mixture is smooth. You will need to soak the almonds overnight, and if you struggle to buy frozen mango or pineapple, peel and chop up the fruit the night before and freeze it.

1 lemon

375ml coconut water, preferably raw (unpasteurised)

1cm piece of fresh ginger, peeled and roughly chopped

Handful of almonds, soaked overnight, or for at least 6 hours, and rinsed

Big handful of kale, thick stalks discarded, leaves roughly chopped or torn

1 teaspoon green powder of your choice (optional)

1 ripe medium banana, cut or broken into chunks

200–220g frozen fruit (e.g. pineapple and mango)

Cut the lemon in half then cut a thick slice off one half. Chop this up roughly and place in a blender. Squeeze the juice from the remaining lemon halves and add, together with the coconut water, ginger and almonds, to the blender. Blend until smooth.

Add the rest of the ingredients and blend until smooth and creamy. If your blender allows for the use of a tamper, it is a good idea to press the frozen fruits down into the blade to avoid uneven blending.

3. Pumpkin pie

According to my husband, this smoothie has it all. It's a great way to use up leftover butternut squash, pumpkin or sweet potato and is a wonderful breakfast or late-afternoon snack.

Finely grated zest of 1 small orange

250ml freshly squeezed orange juice (about 3 oranges) (or half milk of your choice, and half orange juice)

½ small Dolce Verde romaine lettuce heart, trimmed and roughly chopped

2 pitted large Medjool dates

80g cooked butternut squash (or pumpkin or sweet potato)

1 tablespoon peanut (or other nut) butter

Large pinch of ground cinnamon

A few pinches of freshly grated nutmeg

Handful of ice cubes

Blend the orange zest, juice, lettuce and dates until smooth. Add the rest of the ingredients, except the ice cubes, and blend until smooth.

Add the ice and blend one last time until smooth.

Left to right, from back: Pumpkin pie smoothie;
Ultimate green smoothie; The pick-me-up smoothie

Creamy cavolo nero and shiitake mushroom soup

I love this one. It is perhaps not surprising that it tastes wonderful, given the added cream, but if you are able to find unpasteurised dairy from pastured animals, it needn't be a guilty pleasure, especially as both cavolo nero (also called lacinato, Tuscan kale or black cabbage) and shiitakes are considered extremely health-supportive. For the crispy shiitake, use large mushrooms, as they shrink considerably while baking. SERVES 4

Carefully toss the mushrooms for the crispy shiitake with the salt and smoked paprika, then spread out in a single layer on a baking tray lined with baking parchment. Drizzle with the olive oil, ensuring most mushrooms receive some. Leave to stand for at least 15 minutes to allow the spices to penetrate. Meanwhile, preheat the oven to 160°C/320°F/Gas 3.

Bake the mushrooms for 20–30 minutes or until they have shrunk considerably and are crispy around the edges, rotating the baking tray once during cooking and keeping an eye on them towards the end to avoid burning. Remove from the oven and set aside to cool.

Meanwhile, put the dried mushrooms in a small bowl and add enough warm water to cover. Leave to soak for 15 minutes.

Gently heat the oil in a large saucepan, add the onion and sweat over a low heat for a few minutes until soft and translucent. Add the sliced fresh shiitakes and fry over a relatively high heat until cooked and slightly caramelised.

Add the soaked mushrooms with their liquid, the cavolo nero, sweet potato and stock, and simmer for about 20 minutes until the sweet potato is tender.

Blend the soup until smooth and velvety, then return it to the pan and stir in nearly all the cream, keeping some back to serve. Keep the soup hot, but don't let it boil once the cream has been added.

Season with lemon juice, salt and black pepper, and serve with a drizzle of porcini oil, a splash of cream and the crispy shiitake.

10g dried wild mushrooms

Splash of extra virgin olive oil

1 medium onion, roughly chopped

125g fresh shiitake mushrooms, stems removed, sliced

200g cavolo nero, thick stems removed, roughly chopped

1 medium-sized sweet potato, peeled and cut into large dice

500ml vegetable or fresh chicken stock

500ml single cream (cow's, goat's, or sheep's), plus extra for garnish

Squeeze of lemon juice, to taste

Sea salt and freshly ground black pepper

Porcini oil, to serve

FOR THE CRISPY SHIITAKE
125g large fresh shiitake mushrooms, stems removed, thinly sliced

Pinch of fine sea salt

1 teaspoon smoked paprika

1 tablespoon olive oil

Spring greens and smoked haddock soup with watercress snow

This is a very hearty, warming soup and definitely a proper meal-in-one. It is also quite kid-friendly, and easy to prepare in advance up to the step of adding the fish. The watercress snow makes enough to serve 8, but the surplus will keep well in the freezer for at least a couple of months. You need to make it the day before, to allow for freezing time. SERVES 4

In a small food processor, blitz all the ingredients, except the olive oil, for the watercress snow, scraping down the sides a few times, then stir in the olive oil until it just reaches a sauce-like consistency.

Transfer to a flat, shallow container and place in the freezer for at least 6 hours.

When you are ready to make the soup, heat the oil or butter in a large saucepan over a medium heat, add the leek, celery, onions and garlic with a pinch of salt and sweat until soft and translucent. Add the potatoes and cook a little longer, resisting the urge to stir.

Add the stock, wine, ground fennel and bay leaves, and bring to the boil. Reduce the heat and simmer for about 20 minutes with the lid ajar until the potatoes are tender.

Remove the bay leaves and blend the soup until smooth. Add salt and pepper to taste, and a little hot water if it is too thick. Return the soup to the pan and stir in the greens. Simmer until tender, then either remove half the soup and blend again, or use a stick blender to partially blend the soup in the pan; you want a smooth soup with bits of greens to chew on.

Add the fish and simmer for a few minutes until it is cooked through or flaky. Be careful not to overcook it, as it will become dry and stringy.

While the fish is cooking, remove the watercress snow from the freezer and cut half into chunks (return the rest to the freezer for another occasion). Process the chunks in a blender to make a frozen powder, or use a sharp knife to chop it up.

Serve the soup hot with lots of watercress snow and the reserved toasted, chopped almonds.

A little olive or coconut oil, or butter

1 leek, trimmed, sliced in half lengthways and sliced across into half-moons

2 celery stalks, trimmed and roughly chopped

2 medium onions (about 200g), roughly chopped

2 large garlic cloves, roughly chopped

2 large potatoes (about 400g), peeled and cut into medium dice

1 litre fish or vegetable stock

125ml dry white wine (or extra stock)

1 teaspoon fennel seeds, toasted in dry frying pan for 1–2 minutes until fragrant, then finely ground

2 bay leaves

300g (1 medium bunch) spring or collard greens, very finely shredded

300g undyed smoked haddock fillet, cut into bite-sized pieces

Sea salt and freshly ground black pepper

FOR THE WATERCRESS SNOW
100g watercress

60g almonds, toasted in hot oven for 7–8 minutes (reserve half for garnish)

Squeeze of lemon juice

1 garlic clove, finely chopped

Pinch each of sea salt and freshly ground black pepper

1–2 tablespoons extra virgin olive oil

Green gazpacho

Gazpacho always reminds me of the disappointed look on my dad's face the first time he had this traditional Spanish soup. He loves all things tomato, but did not expect something cold... Since then we have all grown to love cold soups during the hot summer months. They are wonderful for entertaining, as they can be prepared in advance. If you have more ripe avocados than you need here, dice them, toss with lime juice and scatter over the soup before adding the ice cubes. Another option is to serve it with chopped chives or dill and a dollop of sour cream. SERVES 4

Start preparing this recipe the day before you intend to serve this soup. For the ice cubes, juice the cucumber (or blend and strain through a nut milk bag or several layers of muslin), then stir in the lime juice and season generously with salt and pepper. Fill each cavity of the ice tray with the cucumber juice, then place a small edible flower or mint leaf in each. Freeze overnight. The dark green bits will sink to the bottom, creating a beautiful colour contrast when the cubes start to melt in each bowl of soup.

The next day, juice the cucumbers, celery, apple and spring onions. Alternatively, you could use a powerful blender and strain the pulp through a few layers of muslin or a nut milk bag.

Transfer to a clean blender, add the lime juice and avocados and blend until smooth. Add the Worcestershire sauce with Tabasco, lemon juice, salt and pepper to taste.

Serve on a hot day with a few cucumber ice cubes added to each serving.

2 large cucumbers, peeled and roughly chopped

2 celery stalks, chopped

1 large green apple, chopped

2 spring onions, cut into quarters

Juice of 1–2 limes, to taste

2 small avocados (about 250g), peeled and cubed

1 tablespoon Worcestershire sauce

Tabasco, to taste

Squeeze of lemon juice

Sea salt and freshly ground black pepper

FOR THE ICE CUBES
1 cucumber

Juice of 1 lime

Edible flowers, such as borage, or small mint leaves

Sea salt and black pepper

Pumpkin and tamarind soup

This is a delicious North African-inspired soup that would make a great starter course, but is equally good as a light meal with some flatbread and hummus. Tamarinds are tart fruits often used as a spice and souring agent in South Asian, but also North African, dishes. They are rich in tartaric acid (a powerful antioxidant), several minerals and vitamins, and contain many volatile phytochemicals with medicinal properties. SERVES 4

Heat a little coconut oil in a large saucepan and brown the diced pumpkin in batches. You are looking for some caramelisation on the surfaces.

Put all the pumpkin back into the pan with the garlic, leek and ginger and sauté for another couple of minutes, taking care not to burn the garlic.

Now add the stock and tamarind paste and simmer for 5–10 minutes, or until the pumpkin is just tender. Add the pak choy stalks and continue to cook until these, too, are tender.

Remove the pan from the heat and add the orange juice. Blend until smooth using a blender or stick blender. Stir in the chopped coriander. Keep warm, but don't allow to boil.

For the spice oil, heat the coconut oil in a small saucepan until hot but not smoking. Add the mustard seeds and fry until they start to pop (a couple of minutes). Add the chilli flakes and cumin seeds and cook until fragrant (another couple of minutes). Add the ground coriander and turmeric and cook for a minute longer.

Lastly, stir the pak choy leaves and most of the spice oil into the hot soup, and serve garnished with a sprig of fresh coriander and a drizzle of spice oil.

Coconut oil, for frying

1.2kg pumpkin (or butternut squash), peeled and cut into large cubes (should yield 900g–1kg)

2 large garlic cloves, finely chopped

1 leek, trimmed, halved lengthways and sliced into half-moons

1 heaped tablespoon freshly grated ginger

580–625ml vegetable or fresh chicken stock

2 tablespoons tart tamarind paste

300g pak choy, stalks and leaves separate

Juice of 1 orange (about 40ml)

Small bunch of fresh coriander, finely chopped (reserve a few sprigs to garnish)

FOR THE SPICE OIL
2 tablespoons coconut oil

2 teaspoons yellow mustard seeds

½–1 teaspoon dried chilli flakes (or more, to taste)

3 teaspoons cumin seeds

3 teaspoons ground coriander

1 teaspoon ground turmeric

Spinach, broccoli and lentil soup with Stilton croûtons

Green vegetables are so beautiful when puréed or blended! They owe their vibrant colour to chlorophyll, a green pigment instrumental in the process of photosynthesis that has many health benefits when consumed. Usually the colour starts to become faded after exposure to heat for more than 10 minutes. So, to ensure your soup retains its glorious hue, I suggest cooking the lentils separately first, but if this is too much of a faff, just add them to the soup after you have blended it. SERVES 4

Soak the lentils in four times their volume of cold water for at least 6 hours, or overnight.

Preheat the oven to 160°C/320°F/Gas 3. If using bacon, place a wire rack inside a lipped baking tray and lay the bacon rashers on top. Bake in the oven for 20–30 minutes, until crispy around the edges. Remove them using tongs, blot any excess fat with kitchen paper, cut into small strips and set aside.

For the croûtons, toss the bread cubes in a little olive oil, season with salt and pepper, and place closely together on a lipped baking sheet. Scatter over the crumbled blue cheese, being careful to keep most of the cheese on the bread and not on the sheet. Bake for 15 minutes or until crunchy, then remove from the oven and allow to cool.

If cooking the lentils separately (see Introduction above), drain them and put into a small saucepan with double their volume of fresh water, the garlic clove and bay leaf. Bring to the boil, then reduce the heat, cover and simmer for 15 minutes or until they are just tender.

Meanwhile, heat the oil in a soup pan and gently cook the leeks, celery and broccoli stems until just tender, 5–10 minutes, depending on thickness.

Add the broccoli florets, most of the stock (reserving some to adjust the consistency of the soup at the end) and all the spices. Simmer, uncovered, for about 5 minutes until all the vegetables are tender.

Stir in half the spinach and remove from the heat as soon as it has wilted. Blend the soup with the remaining spinach until completely smooth.

Return to the pan and add the lentils. If you didn't cook the lentils separately, simmer, uncovered, for another 15 minutes, or until lentils are just cooked. Adjust the seasoning and add a little more stock if the soup is too thick.

Stir in the bacon, if using, and serve topped with cheesy croûtons.

100g dried green lentils

200g unsmoked bacon rashers (optional)

1 garlic clove, crushed, and 1 bay leaf (only if cooking the lentils separately)

A glug of extra virgin olive oil

2 medium leeks (about 400g), trimmed, halved lengthways and sliced into half-moons

3 celery stalks, trimmed and roughly chopped

320–340g broccoli, stem finely chopped and florets roughly chopped

1.2 litres hot vegetable stock

Pinch of cayenne pepper

¼ teaspoon ground allspice

Seeds of 5 cardamom pods

200g spinach, washed

FOR THE CROÛTONS
150g sourdough bread (2–3 thickish slices from a large loaf), cut into cubes

Extra virgin olive oil

50–60g Stilton or other blue-veined cheese, crumbled

Sea salt and freshly ground black pepper

Watercress, pea and sweetcorn soup with mint and onion popcorn

This is one of my absolute favourites, with the mountain of white popcorn gloriously set off against the greenest of greens. SERVES 4

Heat a tiny bit of butter, ghee or olive oil in a saucepan and gently sweat the onion with a large pinch of salt until soft and translucent. Add the celery and cook for another few minutes before adding the garlic.

Cook for another minute or so, then add half the peas and half the sweetcorn kernels, with the split peas and stock. Bring to the boil, then reduce the heat and simmer gently for 20–25 minutes, until the split peas are tender.

While the soup is cooking, make the popcorn. Heat the oil or butter in deep saucepan and scatter the popcorn over the base. Cover with a lid and wait for a few minutes until they start to pop.

Meanwhile, mix together the melted butter, salt, mint and garlic powder. As soon as the popping has slowed down significantly, pour this mixture over the popcorn. Remove from the heat, cover with the lid and give the pan a few good shakes. Set aside.

As soon as the split peas are tender, add the watercress and cook just until the leaves wilt. Remove from the heat and add the milk and mint leaves.

Blend until smooth, then return to the pan, stir in the remaining peas and sweetcorn and season with salt and pepper. Reheat briefly and gently before serving.

Serve the soup in bowls topped with a mound of popcorn, some shredded mint and the remaining spice crumbs from the bottom of the popcorn pan. Don't stir the popcorn into the soup as you eat it, as it will turn soggy and not be nearly as much fun to eat.

Butter, ghee or olive oil

1 medium onion, chopped

2 celery stalks (about 120g trimmed weight), roughly chopped

1 large garlic clove, chopped

110g peas, fresh or frozen

1 ear of sweetcorn, kernels sliced off

125g yellow split peas, rinsed

625–750ml vegetable stock

200g watercress, leaves and stalks

375ml full-cream milk or milk substitute, such as almond or coconut milk

Large handful of mint leaves

Sea salt and freshly ground black pepper

FOR THE POPCORN

1½ teaspoons coconut or rapeseed oil, or butter

40g popping corn, preferably organic

2 teaspoons melted butter

Pinch of sea salt

1 teaspoon finely shredded mint leaves, plus extra to serve

½ teaspoon dried garlic powder or granules

Rich tomato broth with chard, borlotti beans and parsley pistou

This is a good example of a recipe that can be altered to suit your mood, available time and audience. It seems complicated, but really doesn't take much time at all. You could blend the broth and the rest of the cooked vegetables for a thick and hearty vegetable soup, particularly good with some sour cream stirred through. The parsley pistou provides an essential hit of freshness and flavour. SERVES 4–6

For the broth, gently heat the oil in a saucepan, add the onion, celery and carrot with a large pinch of salt and cook for a few minutes until the onion is soft and translucent. Add the garlic and dried herbs and cook for another minute or two before adding the rest of the broth ingredients. Bring to the boil, reduce the heat slightly and simmer, uncovered, for 30 minutes.

Meanwhile, for the soup, use a vegetable swivel peeler to remove the outer layer of the fennel bulb. Separate the bulb into layers and chop each layer into small dice.

When the broth is ready, allow to cool slightly before straining through a sieve. Use the back of a large metal or wooden spoon to press the vegetables down in the sieve and squeeze out every last bit of liquid, which will help to give the broth some body. Discard the pulp.

Return the broth to the pan, season with salt and pepper, then add the diced potatoes and carrot. Cover and simmer for about 5 minutes, or until the potatoes are very close to tender.

Add the fennel, chard stalks and courgette, cover and simmer for another few minutes, or until the chard stalks are tender. Stir in the shredded chard leaves and simmer, uncovered, for a few minutes, before adding the broad beans or peas, with the cooked borlotti beans. Remove from the heat once the peas and borlotti beans are heated through. Do not leave on the heat for too long at this stage, or the greens and peas lose their lovely bright green colour.

Serve immediately with a large dollop of Parsley Pistou and some sourdough toast.

1 quantity of Parsley Pistou (page 41)

FOR THE BROTH
2 tablespoons extra virgin olive oil

1 onion, finely chopped

2 celery stalks, finely chopped

1 small carrot, scrubbed clean and finely chopped

2 garlic cloves, roughly chopped

2 teaspoons dried marjoram or oregano

1kg (about 8 large or 12 small) ripe tomatoes, fibrous core removed and roughly chopped

2 teaspoons tomato purée

Large pinch of unrefined brown sugar

2 bay leaves

1.25 litres hot vegetable stock

Sea salt and freshly ground black pepper

FOR THE SOUP
350g fennel (1 large bulb), trimmed

250g (about 2 medium) potatoes, peeled and cut into small dice

150g (about 1 medium-large) carrot, scrubbed clean and cut into small dice

200g chard, stalks diced and leaves finely shredded

200–250g (1 large or 2 small) courgettes, cut into small dice

110g baby or freshly picked broad beans, or peas

280g cooked borlotti beans (120g dried, see page 152)

Saucy and spreadable greens

Green hummus

I am not a huge fan of canned beans and pulses, as they are too squishy and have not been soaked before cooking, which means they are likely to be less digestible and the nutrients harder to assimilate. Dishes also often taste better with freshly cooked beans, and many recipes call for the bean cooking liquid, which contains the flavour and the starch from the cooked beans. If you are short of time, use drained canned chickpeas and fresh water to thin instead. This recipe makes enough for two medium-large jars – use one immediately and freeze the other. MAKES 500ML

100g cavolo nero, leaves stripped from the stalks

1 large garlic clove, bashed using the side of a large knife, peeled and roughly chopped

270–280g cooked chickpeas (120g dried, see page 152)

2 tablespoons lemon juice

1½–2 tablespoons tahini

½ heaped teaspoon cumin seeds, dry roasted until fragrant, then ground, plus extra to serve

¼ teaspoon cayenne pepper, plus extra to serve

Large pinch of sea salt

Chickpea cooking liquid or water

Extra virgin olive oil, to serve

Briefly steam the cavolo nero leaves, or cook in a very small amount of water, until just wilted and bright green. Refresh under cold running water until cool, then squeeze out the excess water.

In a food processor, blitz the cavolo nero, garlic and cooked chickpeas until finely chopped. Add the lemon juice, tahini, cumin, cayenne and salt and, with the motor running, enough chickpea cooking liquid or water for the hummus to come together, stopping to scrape down the sides as necessary.

If you like a particularly smooth hummus, transfer it to a strong blender and blend until creamy.

Adjust the seasoning and serve with a drizzle of good-quality olive oil, cayenne pepper and a little ground cumin.

Green butter

This butter is as versatile as it gets – delicious on boiled or baked potatoes, stirred through hot rice or couscous, on toast with egg dishes, with steamed greens, green beans, peas or asparagus, on steak, with boiled or barbecued sweetcorn, and on grilled fish. Freeze it in portions to use as and when the desire strikes.
MAKES 1 SMALL LOG – APPROX. 10–15 SLICES

150g unsalted butter, cubed and softened

1 tablespoon extra virgin olive oil

20g (1 small bunch) parsley, leaves only, very finely chopped

15g basil sprigs, leaves only, very finely shredded (see note below)

1 tablespoon finely chopped sage leaves

1 tablespoon finely chopped tarragon leaves

1 large garlic clove, finely chopped

1 tablespoon salted nonpareille (baby) capers, rinsed and finely chopped

Grated zest of 1 lemon

Large pinch of sea salt

Put all the ingredients into a mixing bowl and use an electric whisk to mix well. Alternatively, you could use a food processor, or whisk it all by hand.

Scoop the mixture onto a large rectangular piece of clingfilm and roll it up like a sausage, spinning the contents around while holding on to the ends, to twist them.

Chill in the fridge for at least 4 hours, or until completely firm. Cut off slices to serve as needed, or freeze for later use.

NOTE:
To shred basil, stack the leaves flat on top of each other, then roll into a cigar shape and slice across into shreds. This method minimises bruising of the very delicate leaves, as a chopping action turns the edges black.

PHOTOGRAPHED WITH SPRING GREENS AND PUMPKIN SEED RYE "SOURDOUGH" ON PAGE 138

Parsley pistou

Hardworking parsley is the star of the show in this easy to prepare, yet punchy sauce. Use it in mashed potatoes, with grilled fish, or spread on sandwiches instead of butter. Try adding a drop or two of best-quality orange oil to create something truly uplifting. MAKES ABOUT 250ML

100g (1 large bunch) flat-leaf parsley, leaves only, very finely chopped

1–2 garlic cloves, finely chopped

Grated zest of 1–2 oranges

60ml extra virgin olive oil

Sea salt and freshly ground black pepper

Mix the parsley, garlic and orange zest with some salt and black pepper in a small bowl, then slowly add the olive oil in a steady stream, stirring until you've reached the desired consistency. Add a little more oil if you prefer. Season to taste.

If you have an efficient small food processor, you could skip the step of finely chopping the parsley and use the processor to make the pistou instead.

Aji sauce

This spicy, creamy green sauce was made popular by a host of Peruvian restaurants, who serve it with spit-roasted chicken that has first been marinated in olive oil, lime juice, garlic and spices, then roasted until tender, juicy and crisp-skinned. You can eat it on almost everything, and it makes a wonderful dip or dressing. I particularly like to use it for potato salads and on boiled eggs. MAKES ENOUGH FOR ROUGHLY 10–12 SERVINGS (ABOUT 250ML)

½ romaine lettuce (about 100g), stem trimmed

50g (1 medium bunch) coriander, thickest part of stalks removed

5 spring onions (about 80g), white and green parts, trimmed and roughly chopped

2 jalapeño chillies (all or some of the seeds and membranes removed if you want a less spicy version)

1 garlic clove, peeled

Juice of ½ lemon

60–125ml mayonnaise (see page 154 to make your own, but omit the tarragon)

Sea salt and freshly ground black pepper

Put the lettuce, coriander, spring onions, chillies, garlic and lemon juice with salt and pepper to taste into a blender and blend until very smooth. You might need to scrape down the sides from time to time to help the blender along.

Pour into a small bowl and whisk in the mayonnaise until the taste and thickness are to your liking. Adjust the seasoning. Store in an airtight container in the fridge for up to 1 week.

PHOTOGRAPH ON PAGE 42

Orange, dill and fennel dressing

This is ideal for dressing a seafood salad or a celeriac remoulade to accompany grilled fish, but also really delicious as a dressing for crunchy coleslaws or a rocket and roasted beetroot salad. MAKES 250–350ML

1 whole fennel bulb, outer layer peeled with a vegetable swivel peeler

Knob of butter or a little oil

180ml fresh orange juice (about 2–3 oranges)

1 tablespoon cider vinegar

1 tablespoon extra virgin olive oil

Large pinch of sea salt

1 teaspoon Dijon mustard

½ teaspoon aniseeds, dry roasted and ground (optional)

20g (1 small bunch) dill, tough stems removed, finely chopped

Cut the fennel bulb lengthways into quarters, then steam in a little water until tender.

Heat the butter in a small pan over a medium heat until frothy, then add the cooked fennel, cut sides down. Leave to caramelise without moving or turning them, until browned around the edges. Remove from the heat and set aside to cool.

Once the fennel has cooled slightly, blend with the orange juice, vinegar, olive oil, salt, mustard and aniseed, if using.

Stir in the chopped dill and adjust the seasoning.

Thai dressing

This spicy little number is the perfect dressing for crunchy slaws or noodle salads, or to add some zing to steamed rice, as well as to briefly marinate chicken or fish, and to drizzle over grilled meat. It freezes well. MAKES ABOUT 125ML

1 tablespoon roughly chopped, peeled galangal (or ginger)

1 red chilli, trimmed and roughly chopped (use a Thai chilli if you like it very spicy)

2 lemongrass stalks, trimmed, tough outer layers removed, roughly chopped

1 garlic clove, peeled and bashed with the back of a knife

2 medium spring onions, trimmed, green and white parts roughly chopped

Juice of 2 limes (about 3½ tablespoons)

2 teaspoons fish sauce

2 teaspoons tamari or shoyu

2 tablespoons untoasted (virgin) sesame oil or extra virgin olive oil

25g (1 small bunch) coriander, stems and leaves

50g (1 medium bunch) mint, leaves only

1 heaped tablespoon palm sugar (or dark muscovado), or to taste

Put all the ingredients in a blender and blend until smooth.

Left to right: Thai dressing; Orange, dill and fennel dressing; Aji sauce (recipe on page 41)

Spinach and caramelised onion dip

This is delicious with potato or vegetable crisps, tortilla chips, pitta chips or crackers. It could also be stirred through hot pasta or mixed with potato mash. A dollop on the bread roll under burger patties works surprisingly well, and it makes a good omelette when stirred into beaten eggs. Try increasing the amount of cream cheese and filling cannelloni, pasta shells or ravioli with it. If you leave out the cream cheese to keep it vegan and dairy-free, add a tablespoon or two of olive oil. Finally, you could leave out the cream cheese, not process the ingredients and serve it as a side dish. It freezes well. MAKES 400–500ML

15g butter

3 medium onions (300–350g), cut in half through the root, then peeled and cut into 5mm half-moon slices

Large pinch of sea salt

¼ teaspoon ground cloves

200g spinach

200g cooked borlotti beans (see page 152)

1–2 tablespoons lemon juice (about 1 small lemon), to taste

50g light cream cheese, softened

Freshly ground black pepper

Heat the butter in a large saucepan over a medium to low heat until just melted, then add the onions, salt and ground cloves. Cook until soft and translucent, for about 5 minutes, stirring regularly. Do not allow the edges to darken or burn, as this will hinder caramelisation.

Turn the heat up to medium and cook for at least 30 minutes, stirring occasionally, until caramelised. If the onions seem to be drying out, stir in a splash of water. Scrape into a food processor.

In the same pan, sauté the spinach until wilted. Let it cool slightly, then squeeze out any excess liquid. Add the spinach and the rest of the ingredients to the food processor with the onions, and process until smooth.

Asparagus and goat's curd spread

This is very good as a dip for pitta chips or as a filling for crêpes, sandwiches, and omelettes served with roasted tomatoes. If you would like to use it as a pasta sauce, reserve the asparagus tips for serving and add a few tablespoons of the pasta cooking liquid to create a sauce-like consistency. MAKES ABOUT 300ML

1 bunch (about 450g) of asparagus spears, trimmed

Olive oil

1 teaspoon butter

1½ tablespoons shredded sage leaves

2 (about 100g) echalion (banana) shallots, finely diced

1½–2 tablespoons lemon thyme leaves, finely chopped

Grated zest of 1 lemon

50g soft fresh goat's curd or rindless soft goat's cheese

1 tablespoon lemon juice (about ½ lemon)

Sea salt and freshly ground black pepper

Preheat the oven to 160°C/320°F/Gas 3.

Toss the asparagus in olive oil to coat and season with some salt. Spread out on a lipped baking tray and roast in the oven for 20 minutes, or until just tender. Set aside to cool.

Meanwhile, heat the butter in a medium saucepan and add the shredded sage leaves. Cook for a few minutes, then increase the heat, add the diced shallots and cook until they begin to brown around the edges.

Add the chopped thyme and cook for another minute or two, then set aside to cool completely.

Put all the ingredients into a food processor, including the cooled asparagus and shallot mixture, with salt and pepper to taste, and process until smooth. If you want it really smooth, use a blender. Adjust the seasoning and serve or store in a jar in the fridge for up to 1 week.

Clockwise from top: Spinach and caramelised onion dip;
Nettle and artichoke pâté (recipe on page 46); Asparagus
and goat's curd spread

Nettle and artichoke pâté

Stinging nettles are usually associated with painful encounters, not edible joys. But set aside your prejudices and try this recipe; you will be most surprised! Although the flavour is quite special, nettles can be hard to find, so feel free to use spinach (especially large leaf) instead – just be sure to squeeze out the excess moisture after cooking. If you are a vegan or avoiding dairy, omit the Parmesan and add 1 teaspoon nutritional yeast flakes. MAKES ABOUT 250ML

70g nettle tips (or large-leaf spinach)

1 garlic clove

Large pinch of sea salt

30–45ml lemon juice (1 lemon)

170g drained artichoke hearts in olive oil (about 280g with the oil)

50g pine nuts, toasted until golden

50g grated Parmesan cheese

Small handful of fresh mint leaves, finely shredded

60ml extra virgin olive oil

Freshly ground black pepper

Bring a pan of water to the boil. Wearing gloves, transfer the nettle tips to the boiling water and blanch very briefly until wilted. Drain and allow to cool, then squeeze out the water and roughly chop.

With a mortar and pestle, grind the garlic clove with the salt until you have a paste.

Add all the ingredients except the olive oil to a food processor and process until smooth. With the motor running, pour in the olive oil in a thin and steady stream until well incorporated.

The end result yields a firm, spreadable pâté. If you would like something a little looser, to stir through pasta or use as a dip for crisps, add a tablespoon or two of water and mix again. When cooking pasta, reserve some of the cooking liquid to thin down the sauce.

PHOTOGRAPH ON PAGE 45

Four-herb pesto

This is a vegan version of the popular sauce known and loved in many different cultures. I keep a jar of it in my fridge at all times, and if any meal lacks flavour, chlorophyll, or a hit of freshness, this is my trusty go-to. Spread on rye bread, serve with grilled fish, combine with a little yoghurt to make a dressing, mix into rice and lentil salads, or mash with avocado for an alternative to guacamole. MAKES ABOUT 500ML

100g (1 large bunch) fresh flat-leaf parsley

100g (1 large bunch) fresh coriander

200g (2 large bunches) fresh basil

60g fresh dill sprigs

1 fat garlic clove, peeled

40g shelled, unroasted macadamia nuts, soaked for a couple of hours, then rinsed

40g shelled, unroasted pistachios, soaked for a couple of hours, then rinsed

40g pine nuts, lightly toasted

125–250ml extra virgin olive oil

Juice of 1 lemon

Sea salt and freshly ground black pepper

Wash all the herbs and remove the toughest stalks. Dry them separately in a salad spinner, or use a clean tea towel to bundle up a small bunch of herbs at a time and spin it around.

Put the parsley and garlic into a food processor, and process, then add each of the remaining herbs in order (coriander, basil, then dill), processing between each addition. Add all the nuts and some salt and pepper, and process.

With the motor running, add enough olive oil in a thin, but steady, stream until the mixture reaches the desired consistency.

Stir in the lemon juice, adjust the seasoning (it needs a fair amount of salt and pepper) and transfer to clean jars. Pour a thin layer of olive oil over the surface of each to seal, put the lids on and store in the fridge. Covered in oil, it will keep for several weeks. Alternatively, freeze.

Rocket and almond green sauce

This pungent sauce with a complex flavour is good stirred through pasta, spooned onto grilled fish or chicken, or used to dress a summery peach and mozzarella salad. Use less oil to make a spread that is perfect on pizza bases, or for sandwiches with soft fresh cheese and tomato. You could also stir some Greek yoghurt through it to make a salad dressing. MAKES ABOUT 250ML

2 medium, hard-boiled egg yolks

About 125ml extra virgin olive oil

60g (1 bunch) wild or regular rocket

50g (1 medium bunch) parsley

Small handful of fresh mint leaves

25g (1 bunch) chives

1 large garlic clove, chopped

60g shelled, unsalted almonds, roasted in a 160°C/320°F/Gas 3 oven for about 10 minutes

1 teaspoon dried chilli flakes, or to taste (optional)

1–2 teaspoons cider vinegar (or other light vinegar)

Sea salt and freshly ground black pepper

Mash the egg yolks with 1 teaspoon of the olive oil until you have a smooth paste. Set aside.

Wash the rocket and all the herbs, discarding the toughest stalks from the rocket and parsley, and dry separately in a salad spinner or a clean tea towel.

Put the rocket and parsley into a food processor and process, then add the mint, chives, garlic and almonds, and process again. When relatively smooth, add the chilli flakes, if using, egg yolk paste, vinegar, a very larch pinch of salt and some pepper, and process for a few more seconds.

With the motor running, add the rest of the oil in a thin, steady stream until it reaches the desired consistency. You may need more, depending on your preferred consistency and how you plan to use it.

Transfer to a clean jar, pour a thin layer of olive oil over the top to seal, put the lid on and store in the fridge for up to 2 weeks. Alternatively, freeze.

Chimichurri

Chimichurri, originally from Argentina, is a very popular green sauce served with all kinds of grilled meats. It is quite simply delicious, and most people – once they have tasted it – admit to eating it on everything, not just meats. The acid in the sauce will turn the herbs a faded green after a couple of days, so eat is as soon as possible after making it and freeze any leftovers. The herbs are traditionally chopped by hand, which can seem quite tedious, but does ensure a lovely texture. If you are pressed for time, though, use a food processor. MAKES 300–350ML

4 medium garlic cloves

Pinch of rock salt

100g (1 large bunch) flat-leaf parsley, leaves only, finely chopped

50g (1 medium bunch) coriander, thickest stalks removed, finely chopped

2 tablespoons finely chopped oregano leaves (or 2 teaspoons dried)

2 tablespoons red wine vinegar

2 tablespoons lemon juice (½–1 lemon)

1 red chilli, finely chopped (remove seeds and membranes for a milder version) or ½ teaspoon dried chilli flakes

1 tablespoon finely chopped shallot (about ½ medium echalion/banana shallot)

Large pinch of sea salt

180–250ml mild extra virgin olive oil

Peel the garlic and grind to a paste with the rock salt, using a pestle and mortar. Transfer to a bowl, add the remaining ingredients except the olive oil, and mix together.

Slowly pour in the oil in a thin, steady stream while stirring, until it reaches the desired consistency.

PHOTOGRAPH ON PAGE 48

Salsa verde

A timeless classic, salsa verde is delicious with almost everything, but feel free to add a handful of chopped mint leaves and some finely chopped rosemary and replace the lemon juice with red wine vinegar when serving it with lamb. A teaspoon of Dijon mustard also works well, and a tablespoon of chopped tarragon is good when serving it with chicken. Salsa verde is best when the herbs are finely chopped by hand, so resist using a food processor. MAKES ABOUT 250ML

25g (1 small bunch) basil, leaves only

50g (1 medium bunch) flat-leaf parsley, leaves only, very finely chopped

1 large or 2 small garlic cloves, finely chopped

2 tablespoons capers, rinsed and chopped

5 anchovy fillets in olive oil, mashed with a fork

About 125ml extra virgin olive oil

3 tablespoons lemon juice (about 1 lemon)

Sea salt and freshly ground black pepper

Working in batches, shred the basil leaves – see Note on page 40 for the best method.

Put the herbs, garlic, capers and anchovies into a bowl and mix well. Add the olive oil slowly, until it reaches desired consistency. Add the lemon juice with salt and pepper to taste, bearing in mind the anchovies are salty already.

Salsa d'agresto

The word agresto in this traditional sauce from Italy means verjuice (juice from unripe grapes), but I have added green grapes and a couple of anchovies instead to create a delicious, moreish sauce. In Italy it is served with grilled meat and fish, and I eat it on almost everything from roast chicken and pan-fried fish, to crostini with cream cheese or ricotta ravioli. MAKES ABOUT 250ML

50g shelled, unroasted walnuts

50g shelled, unroasted pecan nuts

2 anchovy fillets in olive oil

1 garlic clove, peeled

25–30g (1 small bunch) flat-leaf parsley, leaves only, finely chopped

Grated zest and juice of 1 lemon

Pinch of sea salt, or to taste (the anchovies are quite salty)

Freshly ground black pepper, to taste

200g seedless green grapes, washed and finely chopped

125ml extra virgin olive oil

Taste the walnuts: if they are slightly bitter, use only pecan nuts, or soak them in water for a couple of hours, drain and rinse before using.

Depending on the size of your mortar or suribachi, pound about a third or half of the nuts gently until they start to break up. Add the rest of the nuts and repeat. You should end up with a very grainy texture. Do not over-grind.

Add the anchovies and garlic and continue to pound with the pestle until you have a chunky consistency similar to wet, coarse sand.

Transfer the mixture to a bowl and stir in the rest of the ingredients, except the olive oil. Finally, while stirring continuously, incorporate the olive oil in a thin, steady stream. Adjust the seasoning. Store in an airtight container in the fridge for up to 1 week.

Clockwise from top: Salsa d'agresto; Chimichurri (see recipe on page 47); Salsa verde

Roasted broccoli dip

Consider regularly offering crudités with a dip such as this one at the start of a meal. Research shows that most hungry kids (big and small!) happily snack on these, dramatically increasing their vegetable intake, and even go on to eat more vegetables during the meal. A win-win situation, if you ask me. You could keep this dip dairy-free by replacing the yoghurt with natural coconut or nut-based yoghurt, available at most healthfood stores. MAKES ABOUT 500ML

Preheat the oven to 160°C/320°F/Gas 3.

Rub both cut halves of the garlic bulb with olive oil. Sprinkle with salt and pepper, then place the cut sides back together and wrap in foil.

Wash the broccoli, then separate into florets and dry thoroughly with a clean tea towel. Toss the florets in some olive oil, salt and pepper and transfer to a baking tray, spreading them out in a single layer.

Roast the broccoli and garlic in the oven for 20–30 minutes until the broccoli is just cooked through and not burnt. Roast the garlic at the same temperature, but for 45–60 minutes, until the cloves are soft enough to squeeze from their skins.

Put the remaining ingredients, with salt and pepper to taste, into a food processor or blender and add the roasted broccoli and squeezed out garlic. Process until smooth, scraping down the sides a few times if necessary.

If you like your dip a little runnier, add small amounts of hot water with the motor running, or more yoghurt.

PHOTOGRAPHED HERE WITH NORI AMARANTH CRACKERS
(RECIPE ON PAGE 136)

1 whole unpeeled garlic bulb, cut in half horizontally

60ml extra virgin olive oil, plus extra for the garlic and broccoli

1 small head of broccoli

175g cooked light-coloured beans, such as butter beans or cannellini (see page 152)

25g (1 small bunch) parsley

25g (1 small bunch) coriander

60ml goat's or cow's yoghurt

Sea salt and freshly ground black pepper

Smoked mackerel and watercress mousse

Serve this as an indulgent appetiser on Watercress Oat Cakes (page 136), or as first course or light lunch with wafer-thin toasted sourdough and the Sea Vegetable Salad (page 119).
MAKES 375ML

Using clingfilm, line a mini loaf tin or a mould that will hold 375ml liquid, making sure the clingfilm hangs over the sides (to help unmould the mousse).

Blitz the watercress in a food processor until fine, then add the smoked mackerel and pulse a few times until roughly chopped. Transfer to a bowl and stir in the sour cream and horseradish sauce. Season with a little salt and plenty of pepper, and set aside.

If using powdered gelatine, whisk the granules into the stock and wine in a small saucepan and allow to soften for 1 minute. Gently heat over a low heat until all the granules have dissolved. Set aside to cool slightly before stirring into the fish and cream mixture.

If using leaf gelatine, submerge the leaves in a bowl of room temperature water and allow to soften for 4–5 minutes. Meanwhile, gently heat the stock and wine in a small pan over a low heat. Drain the softened gelatine sheets, squeeze out the excess water, add to the warm liquid and whisk until fully dissolved. Set aside to cool slightly before stirring into the fish and cream mixture.

If using agar agar, slowly bring the stock and wine to the boil in a pan with the agar agar, whisking continuously. If you heat it too rapidly, the agar will form little beads of hard gel. Once the flakes have completely dissolved, remove from the heat and allow to cool only slightly before stirring into the fish mixture.

Adjust the seasoning, bearing in mind that jelling and refrigeration tend to tone flavours down. Scrape the mixture into the prepared mould, then refrigerate until firm, for at least 4 hours. When the mousse has set, lift it out of the mould with the help of the clingfilm. Place a serving plate face down on the mousse, then flip both over and remove the clingfilm. Serve with lemon wedges and a few watercress sprigs.

PHOTOGRAPHED HERE WITH WATERCRESS OAT CAKES (RECIPE ON PAGE 136) AND SEA VEGETABLE SALAD (RECIPE ON PAGE 119)

50g watercress, stalks and leaves, plus a few sprigs to decorate

100g smoked mackerel

60ml sour cream

60ml horseradish sauce (or see page 156 to make your own)

Enough powdered or leaf gelatine to set 250ml liquid (about 1½ teaspoons powdered or 3 gelatine leaves), or 1½ tablespoons agar agar flakes

80ml fish or vegetable stock

60ml white wine (or more stock)

Sea salt and freshly ground black pepper

Lemon wedges, to serve

Fresh chive ricotta

If you've never had freshly made ricotta, you're in for a treat. The beauty of it is its simplicity and subtle taste, and with vibrant green chive oil, it becomes super versatile. Either mix some oil into the ricotta and use as a topping on crostini or in pasta dishes; or reserve the oil to drizzle over ricotta pancakes or soups. It has to be prepared a day ahead to give the chives a chance to flavour the oil, but it is little effort. The leftover whey from the ricotta can be used in place of water in baking recipes or whizzed into smoothies. MAKES ABOUT 500G RICOTTA AND 125ML CHIVE OIL

For the chive oil, bring a small pan of water to the boil and blanch the chives for 20 seconds, then drain and refresh under cold running water, or tip into a bowl of iced water.

Wrap the chives up in a clean tea towel and swing it around to shake off any excess water, then blend with the oil until the chives have been completely incorporated. Pour into a glass jar, put the lid on and infuse in the fridge for 24 hours. Strain the oil through a nut milk bag or a few layers of muslin to remove any pulp.

To make the ricotta, line a colander with a double layer of muslin and set it over a large bowl. Pour the milk into a large, heavy-based pan that is wider than it is high, and heat gradually over a medium heat until almost boiling. The milk should be foamy and starting to steam and bubble around the edges. If a skin has formed, scoop it off and discard.

Reduce the heat to low and add the lemon juice or vinegar and the salt. Stir gently once or twice to distribute the acid, but don't stir more than twice, as it could result in chewy curds. Leave the milk undisturbed for 10 minutes, after which it should have separated into clumps of milky white curds and thin, watery, yellow whey. Dip a slotted spoon in to check; if you still see a lot of unseparated milk, add another tablespoon of lemon juice or vinegar and wait a few more minutes.

Using a slotted spoon, carefully scoop the big curds out of the pan and into the lined colander. Pour any remaining small curds and the whey through the colander, being careful not to break up the larger ones. Leave the curds to drain for 5–10 minutes, depending on how moist you like your cheese.

Scoop the ricotta into a bowl and whisk in the lemon zest and generous amounts of black pepper, with more salt if it needs it. You can store it in an airtight container in the fridge for a few days at this stage.

Now, you can choose to add the chive oil directly to the ricotta or reserve it all for drizzling. If adding, do so bit by bit, tasting along the way until you are happy with the balance. I usually incorporate 3–4 tablespoons of the oil. Serve immediately, drizzled with more chive oil, a grating of black pepper and some lemon zest, and perhaps a few chilli flakes or sweet paprika.

FOR THE CHIVE OIL
25g (1 bunch) chives, cut into thirds

125ml extra virgin olive oil

FOR THE RICOTTA
2 litres whole milk of your choice (cow's, goat's or sheep's)

60ml lemon juice (1½–2 lemons) or white wine vinegar

1 teaspoon salt

Grated zest of 1 large lemon, plus extra to serve

Freshly ground black pepper and coarse sea salt

Dried chilli flakes or sweet paprika, to serve (optional)

Sideshow greens

Pumpkin, sprout and sage "truffles" with dukkha

My three-year-old wolfs these down, so I can say with confidence that it is a family-friendly recipe. However, it does take time to prepare and is more of a weekend or festive-occasion dish. Be sure to use pumpkin/squash that has a dry flesh, as this will give you a malleable mixture and not a sloppy mess. The dukkha makes about 2 cups of deliciousness to sprinkle on salads, avocado toasties or baked bananas, or to use alongside olive oil as a dip for fresh crusty bread. MAKES ABOUT 24

Preheat the oven to 200°C/400°F/Gas 6.

Toss the pumpkin in the oil or ghee and some salt, then spread out on a baking tray in a single layer and roast for 30–50 minutes, turning the pieces once, until caramelised and dry roasted. If the pumpkin looks as though it is still steaming (or sweating), roast for a further 5–10 minutes. Allow to cool completely before mashing until smooth, then transfer to a bowl.

While the pumpkin is baking, spread the hazelnuts out on a baking tray and roast for 10–15 minutes. Rub between two clean tea towels to remove the skins, then leave to cool.

Finely chop the cooled hazelnuts in the small bowl of a food processor, until there are no large pieces but they still retain lots of texture. Alternatively, use a sharp knife. Mix with all the other dukkha ingredients in a bowl and set aside.

Heat a little oil or ghee in a saucepan and fry the caraway seeds until fragrant. Add the sprouts and cook, stirring regularly, until tender. Tip out onto a chopping board and use a large knife to chop up finely. Mix with the cranberries in the bowl of mashed pumpkin and season generously with salt.

Using a teaspoon, scoop small amounts of pumpkin mixture into your hand and roll into balls. If the mixture still feels too moist to roll into truffles, add a few spoonfuls of quinoa or fine oat flakes until the mixture becomes manageable.

Working in batches, pour some dukkha into a soup bowl and roll the truffles in the dukkha until well covered. Continue until all the truffles are coated, then serve.

FOR THE TRUFFLES

1 medium (about 1kg) dry-fleshed pumpkin or squash (such as onion squash), peeled, seeds removed and cut into medium dice

½ tablespoon grapeseed oil, or melted coconut oil or ghee, plus extra for frying

½ teaspoon caraway seeds

120g Brussels sprouts, trimmed, halved and very thinly sliced

40g dried cranberries, roughly chopped

Sea salt

FOR THE DUKKHA

125g shelled, unroasted hazelnuts

1 tablespoon cumin seeds, toasted in a dry frying pan until fragrant

1 tablespoon ground coriander

50g sesame seeds, toasted in a dry frying pan until golden

1 heaped tablespoon dried mint (or use the contents of a mint tea bag)

2 teaspoons nigella seeds

1 teaspoon sea salt

½ teaspoon freshly ground black pepper (or less if feeding children)

2 teaspoons dulse flakes (optional)

Polenta and Swiss chard chips with rich tomato sauce

This is usually a hit with kids and very easy to make, but requires a little planning ahead. The polenta needs to be made and then cooled completely before being cut and roasted. If you can't find chard, use any dark leafy green of your choice. SERVES 4–6

Cut the stalks off the chard leaves, chop them into small pieces and set aside. Chop the leaves into bite-sized pieces and set aside, separately.

Melt the butter in a large, deep saucepan, add the onion with a pinch of salt and sweat over a medium heat. Add the chard stalks and sauté for 5–10 minutes until tender, then add the leaves and sauté for a minute longer.

Add the boiling water to the pan and stir in the polenta. Whisk until thickened, then stir in 1 teaspoon salt and some pepper, cover and cook over a low heat for 10–20 minutes. Pour into an ovenproof dish and flatten with the back of a metal spoon to an even thickness of about 3cm or, if your dish is large enough, 1.5cm. Leave to set and ideally refrigerate for a few hours.

Preheat the oven to 200°C/400°F/Gas 6.

When the polenta is completely firm, cut into "chips" about 1.5 x 1.5cm thick and 8cm long. Place all the chips on a baking tray close together and brush on all sides with melted coconut oil, ghee or grapeseed oil.

Spread the chips out a little and roast in the oven for about 1 hour, until golden and crunchy on the outside, carefully turning them with a spatula after 30 minutes. Serve hot with the warmed Rich Tomato Sauce.

200g Swiss or rainbow chard, washed well

A little butter

1 medium onion, peeled and finely diced

1.375 litres boiling water

280g medium or coarse polenta

Melted coconut oil or ghee, or grapeseed oil, for brushing

Sea salt and freshly ground black pepper

¼ quantity of Rich Tomato Sauce (page 153), warmed, to serve

Savoury porridge
with oriental greens

If you are in need of a side dish that stands its ground, this is the one. It is earthy and comforting, yet fragrant and cheeky. It sits nicely alongside good pastured meat or line-caught fish, though for me a poached or fried egg is the most perfect partner of all. SERVES 4 GENEROUSLY

For the porridge, put the oats, galangal, salt and lemongrass in a medium saucepan. Add the hot water or stock and the coconut milk. Bring to the boil, then reduce the heat to low and simmer for 30–35 minutes, stirring frequently.

Five minutes before the porridge is ready, for the oriental greens, heat the coconut oil in a wok or large frying pan. When the oil is hot, but before it reaches smoking point, add the spring onions and chillies, cook for 1 minute, then add the garlic and ginger, cooking for another minute while stirring continuously.

Add the mange tout and stir-fry for a minute before adding the greens and salt. Once the greens have wilted, add the broccoli and Thai basil and stir until the basil has wilted. Serve immediately on top of the porridge.

FOR THE PORRIDGE

240g pinhead oats

A few slices of fresh or dried galangal (or ginger)

1 teaspoon sea salt

1 lemongrass stalk, cut into thirds and bashed with the back of a knife

480ml hot water, vegetable stock or fresh chicken stock

600ml coconut milk (about 1½ cans)

FOR THE ORIENTAL GREENS

1 tablespoon coconut oil

4 spring onions, white and green part, trimmed and diagonally sliced

1–2 red chillies, sliced (seeds and membranes removed if you prefer less heat)

2 garlic cloves, finely chopped

1 tablespoon grated peeled ginger

200g mange tout, trimmed and any strings removed

1 small bunch (about 300g) of spring or collard greens

1 teaspoon sea salt

200g purple sprouting, tenderstem or regular broccoli, briefly steamed and refreshed under cold water

25g (1 small bunch) Thai basil (or regular basil), leaves only

Clockwise from left: Wilted spinach and lettuce;
Braised leeks with peas and dill; Broad beans with
sultana and pistachio crumble

Broad beans with sultana and pistachio crumble

This is a family favourite and you will see why once you've tasted it. To double-pod fresh, mature broad beans, remove the beans from the outer pods, then boil them for a couple of minutes and shock under cold water. Next, slip off the grey, leathery skins to reveal the luminous green bean inside. Simply blanch frozen broad beans very briefly in boiling water. SERVES 4–5

300g fresh (or 320g frozen) double-podded broad beans (from approx. 1.25kg beans in their pods)

A few tablespoons of Tarragon Mayonnaise (page 154)

FOR THE CRUMBLE
50g wholemeal spelt flour or gluten-free flour mix

50g cold butter or cold coconut butter, cut into small cubes

25g quinoa flakes or fine oat flakes

Pinch of sea salt

50g shelled, unroasted pistachios

50g sultanas

Preheat the oven to 180°C/350°F/Gas 4.

Put the spelt flour, cold butter, quinoa flakes and salt in a food processor and pulse until it starts to come together. Now add the pistachios and sultanas, and pulse a few more times. Scrape into a bowl and knead a little to form a dough.

Break the dough into large chunks (your aim is crunchy nuggets of crumble the size of granola clusters) onto a lipped baking tray and bake for 20–30 minutes or until the crumble is golden and crispy. Remove and leave to cool.

A few minutes before the crumble is ready, steam the broad beans very briefly to heat. Mix with 2–3 tablespoons Tarragon Mayonnaise and arrange on a plate. Scatter the toasted crumble over and serve immediately as it does not keep very well.

FIRST THREE DISHES PHOTOGRAPHED ON PAGES 64–65

Braised leeks with peas and dill

This is the kind of dish that feels luxurious, although it is easy to make and not at all exotic. SERVES 4–5

15g butter

1 tablespoon extra virgin olive oil, plus extra to drizzle

500g trimmed leeks, halved lengthways, then cut into 10cm pieces

Large pinch of sea salt

1 large fennel bulb, outer layer peeled with a vegetable swivel peeler, halved lengthways and sliced

250ml hot vegetable stock

125ml dry sherry (or extra stock)

½ teaspoon ground aniseed

2 large, thick slices sourdough bread, cut into chunks

150g fresh or frozen peas

10g (½ small bunch) dill, larger stalks removed, finely chopped

Sea salt and freshly ground black pepper

Preheat the oven to 160°C/320°F/Gas 3.

Heat the butter and oil in a large saucepan that will fit the vegetables snugly. Add the leeks, cut sides down, and a large pinch of salt. After a few minutes, turn them over and sauté for another few minutes before adding the fennel, stock, sherry if using, aniseed and some black pepper. Cover and braise over a low heat for 20–30 minutes, or until the leeks and fennel are tender.

Meanwhile, process the bread to coarse crumbs in a food processor, tip onto a lipped baking tray, sprinkle with salt and pepper and a good drizzle of olive oil and spread out in a single layer. Bake for 20–25 minutes or until golden and crunchy.

Using a slotted spoon, transfer the cooked vegetables to a bowl, leaving the sauce in the pan, and keep warm. Simmer the sauce over a high heat for 5–10 minutes until reduced by three-quarters. Stir in the peas and, as soon as they are warm, add the dill. Return the vegetables to the pan and mix.

Top with the crispy sourdough crumbs and serve immediately as it does not keep very well.

Wilted spinach and lettuce

This is one of my favourite recipes in this book, and the type of dish that my kids happily eat if I chop it up finely. The black sesame seeds can be a pain to find if you don't have a good local ethnic grocer near you, but you can use hulled white ones instead. SERVES 2–4

Grapeseed oil or melted coconut oil

1 large shallot, finely chopped

2 Little Gem lettuces, trimmed, leaving the core intact, rinsed and quartered lengthways

1 large or 2 small garlic cloves, finely chopped

200–250g baby leaf spinach

FOR THE DRESSING
1 teaspoon traditionally fermented organic soy sauce, tamari or shoyu (see Note on page 88)

1 teaspoon umeboshi vinegar (also called umeboshi seasoning) or brown rice vinegar

1 teaspoon untoasted (virgin) sesame oil

1 tablespoon white and black sesame seeds, lightly toasted in a dry frying pan until white ones are golden

½ teaspoon honey

Pinch of kombu (kelp) flakes (optional)

½ teaspoon ground Szechuan pepper

1 teaspoon freshly ground nutmeg

Grated zest of 1 tangerine

Make the dressing by combining all the ingredients in a jar and shaking to dissolve the honey.

Heat some oil in a large pan and cook the shallot until soft and translucent. Scrape to the edges of the pan, increase the heat a tad and place the lettuce quarters, cut sides down, in the pan, adding a little more oil if necessary.

When the lettuce pieces have caramelised, turn them over, add the garlic and spinach and keep moving the spinach around as it starts to wilt.

As soon as all the spinach has wilted, pour over the dressing, toss, adjust the seasoning and and serve immediately as it does not keep very well.

Green beans, artichokes and olives

Most people love green beans and I usually serve them as a side in some shape or form. This dish is a little more daring than the usual green bean fare, but feel free to omit the olives if you wish. If you are making this in advance, remember that the acid in the lemon juice will turn the lovely bright-green beans an army green after a little while, so dress the beans just before serving. SERVES 4–6

300g fine green beans, topped and tailed

1 medium garlic clove, finely chopped

1½ tablespoons extra virgin olive oil (if you can find orange-infused olive oil, even better)

1½ tablespoons lemon juice (about ½ large lemon)

175g grilled artichokes in oil, drained and quartered if large

50g Spanish Couchillo olives (or any other small black olives)

Grated zest of 1 orange

Sea salt, to taste (the olives are quite salty)

Steam the beans in a little water until just tender. Drain immediately and refresh under cold running water until completely cooled.

Put the beans with the remaining ingredients in a bowl and toss well to mix.

Flower sprouts with anchovies and roasted garlic

Flower sprouts are a newly developed vegetable that look like tiny cabbages with green frilly leaves and streaks of purple. They are related to Brussels sprouts, but have a more subtle flavour and are richer in vitamins B6 and C. In this recipe you could substitute steamed cavolo nero or other leafy greens for the flower sprouts. SERVES 4

1 tablespoon extra virgin olive oil

3 anchovy fillets in oil

½ quantity of Roasted Garlic (page 154)

250g steamed flower sprouts

Lemon juice, to taste

Sea salt and freshly ground black pepper

Gently heat the olive oil in a large pan and add the anchovies and garlic, squeezed out of its skins. Use a fork to mash both into the oil.

Increase the heat a little, shake off any excess liquid from the steamed flower sprouts and add to the pan. Sauté for a few minutes, add salt and pepper to taste and squeeze over some lemon juice. Serve immediately.

Broccoli and carrot tabbouleh

This is an easy way to get your kids to eat broccoli and an even easier way to make some very basic ingredients taste rather good. You could easily replace the costly pistachios with a seed or nut of your choice. SERVES 4

Glug of good olive oil

1 small onion, finely diced

200–250g finely grated carrot (about 2 medium carrots)

300g (1 small head) broccoli, broken into florets

300g cooked quinoa (about 150g uncooked grain)

90–100g shelled, unroasted pistachio nuts

Sea salt

FOR THE DRESSING
75ml extra virgin olive oil

Juice of 1 lemon (about 2 tablespoons)

Grated zest of 1 lemon

10g (½ bunch) chives, finely chopped

1 garlic clove, finely chopped

½ teaspoon Dijon mustard

1 teaspoon maple syrup

Heat the glug of oil in a saucepan over a gentle heat, add the onion and a pinch of salt and sweat until soft and translucent. Add the grated carrot and cook for a few more minutes.

Blitz the broccoli in a food processor until fine. Add to the onions and cook for another couple of minutes until both the carrot and the broccoli are tender. Transfer to a serving dish.

Combine all the dressing ingredients with a pinch of salt in a glass jar, screw the lid on tightly and give it a good shake.

Pour the dressing over the warm vegetables and mix. Add the quinoa and nuts, mix well and serve. (It is also very good the next day.)

Chinese cabbage kimchi

Please trust me when I say that this is simpler than it looks. Kimchi is chock-full of healthy gut-supportive probiotics and really quite delicious, adding spice and pizzazz to almost anything, from roast chicken or fish, to pancakes and polenta. The method of blending the apple with the spices is something I learnt from food preservationist extraordinaire, Michaela Hayes of Crock & Jar. I have kept this version vegan, so replaced the traditional fish or shrimp sauce with kelp flakes. But do add some sauce if you like – it is more authentic that way. MAKES 1 MEDIUM–LARGE JAR, BUT YOU WILL NEED A LARGE JAR FOR FERMENTATION

Cut the cabbage lengthways into quarters and then across into 4–5cm strips. Put into a large bowl with the salt. Massage the salt into the cabbage until it starts to soften (I usually wear kitchen gloves to do this), then add enough cold water, ideally filtered, to cover the cabbage. Put a plate on top, weigh it down with a few cans and set aside to brine for 2–3 hours.

Rinse the cabbage well under cold water to get rid of most of the saltiness and set aside to drain in a colander for 30 minutes.

Meanwhile, process the garlic, ginger, shallots, apple, tamari, kelp flakes, if using, and water in a small food processor or using a stick blender, until you have a smooth paste. Mix in the gochugaru, using 1 tablespoon for a mild version and up to 5 for a spicy end result (I usually use 2½).

Mix the paste into the carrots, spring onions and radishes. Gently squeeze any remaining water from the cabbage and return it to the bowl along with the vegetables and paste. Mix thoroughly with a large spoon or gloved hands.

Pack the kimchi into a large jar that has ample room at the top to avoid any overflow, pressing down firmly on it until the juices rise to cover the vegetables. On the first day, the liquid might not be quite enough to cover all the vegetables, but it should be by day 2 at the latest. Seal the jar with the lid.

Let the jar stand at room temperature for 2–5 days, checking and tasting it daily, always pressing the vegetables down under the liquid with a clean spoon. Remember to do this at least once a day, as you don't want the gases to build up and the jar to explode. As soon as you like the taste, transfer to the fridge. I prefer my kimchi when it is not overly fermented or "ripe", so usually eat it within a few weeks of transferring it to the fridge, but it keeps well for several months if covered in brine and refrigerated.

1 head (600–650g) of Chinese leaf (you could also use green, white or Savoy cabbage, although the end result will be slightly different)

65g unrefined coarse sea salt

6 garlic cloves

1cm piece of ginger, peeled and grated

2 shallots (about 90g), roughly chopped

1 apple, cored and roughly chopped

2 tablespoons tamari

Large pinch of kelp flakes (optional)

2 tablespoons water

1–5 tablespoons gochugaru (Korean red pepper flakes), or regular dried chilli flakes

3 medium carrots (about 300g), peeled and cut into matchsticks or thin rounds

5 spring onions, green and white parts, trimmed and cut into 5mm slices

150g radishes, trimmed and halved if large

Swiss chard with ginger and tomato sauce

I'll admit this dish is not about the chard. It is about the sauce. Even though the chard (or any wilted leafy green for that matter) tastes great in it, the sauce is also a fantastic overnight marinade for meat, fish or chicken that is destined for the barbecue. The recipe makes more than enough sauce for the chard, but I usually double or triple it to refrigerate or freeze. And if the leftover crystallised ginger is causing you anxiety, try stirring it into pancake or chocolate cake batter, mixing it into cookie dough or adding it to Asian-style vinaigrettes. SERVES 2–4

125ml Rich Tomato Sauce (page 153)

125ml passata

1 tablespoon tomato purée

1 tablespoon grated peeled ginger

¼ teaspoon ground ginger

1 tablespoon (about 15g) finely chopped crystallised ginger

½ teaspoon sweet paprika

½ tablespoon dark muscovado sugar

½ tablespoon lemon juice

Knob of butter or a little coconut oil

300g Swiss chard, washed, stalks chopped and leaves cut into bite-sized pieces

Sea salt

Put all the ingredients except the butter and chard into a small saucepan, add a large pinch of salt and simmer over a low heat for 20–30 minutes, stirring regularly to avoid it catching on the bottom.

Just before the sauce is ready, heat the butter or coconut oil in a pan and sauté the chard stalks with a large pinch of salt until tender. Add the leaves and cook until wilted.

Spoon enough sauce over to coat all the chard. Serve with grilled fish and steamed rice, or alongside a light and fluffy savoury soufflé.

Watercress, mango and avocado salsa

Wonderful with pan-fried or grilled fish or roast chicken, and as an accompaniment to roasted sweetcorn, grilled halloumi or toasted sandwiches, this salsa is a grown-up fruit salad that means business. SERVES 4

1 large, ripe mango (about 500g), diced

2 medium avocados (about 400g), diced

50–60g (about ½ bunch) watercress, leaves picked and stems finely chopped

1–2 red chillies, finely chopped (seeds and membranes removed if you want less heat)

1 small red onion (80–90g), diced

25g (1 bunch) chives, finely chopped

40g (a good handful) dried mango (not the soft, rehydrated kind), cut into thin strips

Sea salt, to taste

Juice of 3 limes (about 3 tablespoons)

Combine all the ingredients in a bowl and stir.

Curried runner bean "tagliatelle"

Inspired by one of my favourite cuisines (Indian) and people (chef Rich LaMarita), this is a characterful side dish for when you need to add some pizzazz to a meal. Fresh curry leaves are now available at most major supermarkets and ethnic grocers. SERVES 4

450g runner beans, sliced lengthways using a bean slicer, or in thirds lengthways using a sharp knife, any strings removed

1 tablespoon coconut oil

½ teaspoon black mustard seeds

½ teaspoon cumin seeds

½ teaspoon black onion seeds (also called kalonji, nigella, black caraway and black cumin seeds)

10–20 fresh curry leaves, depending on size

2 small or 1 large echalion (banana) shallots, halved lengthways and sliced into half moons

1 tablespoon grated peeled ginger

1 garlic clove, mashed to a pulp with some coarse sea salt, using a pestle and mortar

1 red chilli, finely chopped (seeds and membranes removed if you prefer it less spicy)

2 tablespoons creamed coconut (also called coconut manna or coconut butter)

Steam the beans (or boil in very little water) for 8–10 minutes, until tender and no longer crunchy. Refresh under cold running water.

While the beans are steaming, heat the coconut oil in a saucepan large enough to hold the beans, until hot but not smoking. Add the mustard seeds and cook until they just start to pop. Add the cumin and black onion seeds and fry until fragrant. Be careful not to let the spices burn, as they will taste bitter.

While the oil is still very hot, add the curry leaves. They should crackle almost immediately. Add the shallot and sauté for a few minutes before adding the ginger, garlic and chilli.

After a minute or so, add the cooked beans and creamed coconut and stir until the coconut has melted. Season to taste and serve.

Green celeriac mash

I never make plain potato mash any more. Since my aim is always to increase the amount of vegetables our family eats, I mix in mashed swede, grated carrots, puréed cauliflower, and always something green. This version is a great way to up the greens intake without sacrificing flavour. SERVES 4

1 small celeriac (550–600g), peeled and roughly chopped

2–3 medium potatoes or white sweet potatoes (300–350g), peeled and quartered

120g kale, thick stems removed, chopped

1 quantity of Roasted Garlic (page 154)

40g butter

Sea salt

Cook the celeriac and potatoes separately in a little water until tender, adding more hot water after 10 minutes if necessary. Drain.

Meanwhile, steam the kale until wilted, then refresh under cold running water. Blitz in a food processor or finely chop using a very sharp knife.

Squeeze the roasted garlic from its skins into the potatoes, then pass the mixture through a potato ricer or food mill. Use a stick blender or food processor to blend the celeriac until smooth, then mix into the potato mash. Stir in the butter, chopped kale and salt to taste.

Chargrilled courgettes and asparagus with tarragon dressing

I don't often grill or char vegetables; gentle cooking methods are considered most health supportive, as they preserve nutrients. But once in a while it is a lovely alternative to steaming, and the grill marks do add a note of festivity. If you cannot find fresh tarragon, use finely chopped, fresh marjoram or thyme, and add a pinch of ground aniseed. You can make the dressing and grill the vegetables in advance, but keep the elements separate until serving. SERVES 4

Steam the asparagus until just tender. Refresh under cold running water and blot dry with kitchen paper.

Heat a griddle pan until hot. Toss the courgette slices and asparagus spears in a little grapeseed oil and place on the griddle in such a way as to achieve the most attractive grill pattern (allowing for one turn to create a criss-cross effect).

Turn each courgette slice once, and the asparagus spears a couple of times, making sure you don't turn or move the vegetables too early, or you may not get proper grill marks. A few minutes on each side should be about right. Set aside and keep warm. (Alternatively, you can cook the vegetables on a barbecue.)

Meanwhile, mash the garlic with a pinch of coarse sea salt, using a pestle and mortar. Scrape into a glass jar, add the oil, vinegar and mustard with some pepper, screw the lid on tightly and shake until the dressing is mixed well and emulsified. Stir in the herbs.

Toss the griddled vegetables in the dressing and arrange on a serving dish. Scatter over all the toasted almonds and serve immediately.

450g (1 bunch) asparagus (not the tender or fine version), tough part of stalks removed

2 medium courgettes (300–350g), sliced diagonally into 1–1.5cm slices

Grapeseed oil, or cooking oil of your choice

30g flaked almonds, toasted in a dry frying pan until golden

FOR THE DRESSING
1 garlic clove

3 tablespoons extra virgin olive oil

1 tablespoon tarragon vinegar, or cider vinegar

½ teaspoon Dijon mustard

1 tablespoon finely chopped tarragon leaves

1 tablespoon finely chopped chives

1 tablespoon finely chopped parsley

Coarse sea salt and freshly ground black pepper

Main greens

Savoy cabbage and snapper parcels with braised butter beans

This is a lovely dish for when you are having friends round. Prep all your ingredients, then cook the veggies and fish at the same time. Choose small, but thick, pieces of fish (fleshy bourgeois red snapper and monkfish work well) and adjust the spiciness of your bean braise to suit your taste. Remember to remove 5–8 of the largest outer leaves of the cabbage before shredding, as you will need these to make your parcels. SERVES 4

Heat the olive oil for the braised beans in a medium saucepan and sweat the onion with the salt over a medium heat until soft and translucent. Add the celeriac, tomatoes, chilli flakes and a few tablespoons of the bean cooking liquid (or water), and braise, covered, for 10–15 minutes until the celeriac is tender.

Add the shredded cabbage and another tablespoon or two of the bean cooking liquid (or water) and cook for a few minutes until the cabbage is tender. Add the butter beans and samphire and cook for a further 1–2 minutes. Stir in the parsley, set aside and keep warm.

Bring a large pan of salted water to the boil and blanch the large cabbage leaves for a minute or so until tender. Refresh in iced water or under cold running water, then pat dry.

Take the largest cabbage leaf and overlap the two halves to close the gap where the stalk would have been. Place a piece of fish, skin side down, on the leaf, season generously with salt and pepper, put a slice of butter on top, then 2 lemon slices next to each other, and wrap it up like a parcel, using toothpicks or kitchen string to secure the leaf. Repeat with the remaining cabbage leaves and fish ingredients, using 2 overlapping smaller leaves if one is not big enough to wrap the fish.

Place the parcels in a saucepan that fits them snugly in a single layer. Pour in the wine, which should almost cover the parcels, and bring to the boil. Reduce the heat and simmer for 10–15 minutes, or until the fish flakes easily when separated with a fork. You may want to turn the parcels over halfway to ensure both sides are evenly cooked.

To serve, divide the bean mixture between four pasta bowls, drizzle with olive oil, remove the toothpicks from the fish parcels and place them on top. Alternatively, unwrap the fish and shred the cabbage leaf wrappers finely, then mix this into the beans before serving.

NOTE:
The braised beans alone also make a lovely vegan dish. Just add more cabbage and samphire to bulk it up.

FOR THE BRAISED BEANS
2 tablespoons olive oil, plus extra to serve

1 medium onion, diced

Pinch of sea salt

½ celeriac (300–350g), peeled and diced

4 plum or regular tomatoes (300–350g in total), blanched and skinned, quartered, deseeded and diced

Pinch of dried chilli flakes, or to taste

½ Savoy cabbage (300–350g), finely shredded, reserving outer leaves for the parcels

275g cooked butter beans (about 80g dried, see page 152), cooking liquid reserved

60g (large handful) samphire, woody stalks removed (or asparagus, thinly sliced)

2 tablespoons finely chopped parsley

FOR THE FISH
5–8 large Savoy cabbage leaves (see above), thick core removed and top part of leaf left intact

4 thick pieces of bourgeois snapper, 120–140g each, pin-boned

4 thick slices of butter

8 slices of lemon

500ml dry white wine

Sea salt and freshly ground black pepper

Scallops with fennel relish and chunky parsnip mash

If you find fennel a little intimidating, this relish will shine a new light on it. Fennel has become one of my staple vegetables – grated into salads, roasted, lightly steamed. The recipe is a little time-consuming, as it requires lots of chopping, but it is worth the effort and, if you have any relish left over, it is also delicious with cheese and crackers or bean pâté crostini. If you can only find whole ancho chillies, grind them to a powder in a spice grinder or strong blender, or use a sharp knife to chop finely. SERVES 2 (OR 4 AS A STARTER)

For the relish, peel the outer layer of the fennel bulb using a vegetable swivel peeler to get rid of any tough, stringy bits, then separate the layers and cut into small dice. Heat the olive oil in a pan and gently fry the fennel and onion with a pinch of salt until soft. Add the chilli powder and fry for a further 1–2 minutes.

Add the pear and all the citrus juices and simmer over a medium heat, stirring regularly, until the juices have reduced to give a concentrated relish. Season with salt and pepper and stir in the fresh herbs. Set aside.

Meanwhile, cook the parsnips in a little water until tender, then drain and mash using a potato masher. Stir in the lamb's lettuce, olive oil, nutmeg and some salt, then cover and keep warm.

Heat some butter in a cast-iron or other heavy-based frying pan over a medium-high heat until frothy. Season the scallops with salt and black pepper before placing in the hot pan. Fry for 1–2 minutes, then turn them over, reduce the heat a little and cook for a further 1–3 minutes, depending on their size, or until just cooked. Take care not to overcook them.

Serve the scallops on a mound of parsnip mash, topped with the relish.

300–350g (about 4) parsnips, trimmed and roughly chopped

Handful of lamb's lettuce (mâche), roughly chopped

Glug of extra virgin olive oil

Good grating of nutmeg

Butter, for frying

8 scallops

FOR THE RELISH
1 fennel bulb (360–380g), stalks discarded and fronds reserved for garnish

2 tablespoons extra virgin olive oil

2 tablespoons finely chopped red onion

1–2 teaspoons ancho chilli powder

1 large ripe, but not too soft, pear (about 200g), peeled and diced

3 tablespoons tangerine juice (1 tangerine)

3 tablespoons orange juice (about ½ large orange)

1 tablespoon lime juice (1 lime)

2 tablespoons very finely chopped mixture of dill, coriander and/or parsley

Sea salt and freshly ground black pepper

Lamb, mint and coriander burgers

This is one of my favourite ways with minced lamb. Serve with oven-baked, sweet potato fries, a large salad and homemade tomato ketchup or a refreshing tzatziki. The bean sprouts add some crunch to the patties but if you are making these ahead to freeze, omit them. MAKES 4 EXTRA LARGE OR 8 MEDIUM PATTIES

Toast the cumin and coriander seeds in a dry, medium-hot frying pan for a couple of minutes until fragrant. Tip out, allow to cool slightly, then grind with a pestle and mortar or in a spice grinder. Set aside.

Chop the herbs as finely as possible. You could use a small food processor to do this, although I find it less efficient than doing it by hand. Set aside.

Grind the garlic and salt into a paste, using a pestle and mortar. Scrape this into a large mixing bowl and add all the other ingredients. Mix thoroughly with your hands and shape into 4 very large or 8 smaller patties.

Heat a little grapeseed or coconut oil in a large frying pan and fry the patties over a medium to high heat until cooked to your liking – 5–7 minutes each side for the large patties, 4–5 minutes each side for the smaller ones.

1 teaspoon cumin seeds

1 teaspoon coriander seeds

10–15g (small handful) mint, leaves only

25g (1 small bunch) parsley, leaves only

25g (1 small bunch) coriander, largest stalks removed

1 garlic clove, roughly chopped

Generous ½ teaspoon sea salt

500g minced lamb

Pinch of cayenne pepper

Generous grinding of black pepper

1 small onion, finely chopped

1 teaspoon Dijon mustard

1 spring onion, very finely sliced

Large handful of mung bean sprouts, roughly chopped (optional)

Grapeseed or coconut oil, for frying

Portobello mushrooms with cavolo nero and sweet potato

Cavolo nero is a cousin of curly kale and rather delicious; you can substitute one for the other in most recipes. Here I have opted for a mashed, soft mushroom filling, but you could just as well roast the sweet potato until crispy and the mushrooms until tender, roughly chop the cooked cavolo nero and mix everything together to pile on the baked mushrooms, then scatter the grated cheese over and grill for 5–10 minutes. SERVES 2 (OR 4 AS A STARTER)

Preheat the oven to 180°C/350°F/Gas 4.

Remove the mushroom stalks using a small paring knife and season the caps with a little salt and pepper. Place them in an oven dish, gill-side up, that fits them snugly and set aside.

Heat the butter or oil in a saucepan and sweat the onion with a pinch of salt until soft and translucent. Stir in the garlic and, after another couple of minutes, add the chopped cavolo nero. Sauté until wilted and tender. You may want to add a splash of water to help this process along, but then be sure to cook until the saucepan is dry.

Transfer the cavolo and onion mixture to a food processor and process to finely chop (or do this using a large, sharp knife). Transfer to a bowl.

Mash the sweet potatoes with a little butter and salt, add to the cavolo mixture, then stir in the grated cheese, if using, and the sweetcorn.

Divide the mixture equally between the mushroom cavities and smooth the tops. Bake in the oven for 30 minutes or until the mushrooms are tender and the filling is crispy and golden on top.

Just before you are ready to serve, fry, poach or boil the eggs and season with salt and pepper.

Serve the stuffed mushrooms topped with an egg, and with a large green salad alongside.

4 large portobello mushrooms

A little butter or oil

1 medium onion, finely chopped

1 large garlic clove, finely chopped

100g cavolo nero (or regular kale), thick stalks removed, leaves roughly chopped

250g peeled sweet potatoes, cut into medium dice and steamed until just tender

50g mature Cheddar cheese, grated (optional)

1 ear of sweetcorn, kernels cut from the cob

4 eggs

Sea salt and freshly ground black pepper

Spinach and sardine dumplings

Oh my goodness! How much do I love these? They absolutely need to be eaten with lots of the tomato sauce, but as far as serving my family a moreish – and nutritious! – meal, this one is right up there with the best. The mixture or shaped dumplings can be prepared in advance and left in the fridge for a couple of days, making it a good fall-back option for busy evenings. Serve with a fresh green salad. MAKES ABOUT 20

Heat the oil, butter or ghee in a pan, add the onion and sauté until soft and translucent. Add the spinach and cook until wilted.

Squeeze the spinach to get rid of all the excess liquid. Either wear kitchen gloves to do this, or place the spinach in a colander and press against the sides with a large metal spoon (you can keep the water to feed your houseplants and herbs). This step is important; don't be tempted to skip it, or your dumplings will fall apart.

Put the dry spinach, sardines and onion into a food processor and process to a smooth paste. Scrape this mixture into a bowl and mix in the nutmeg, garlic, quinoa or oat flakes, Parmesan, egg white, and a little salt (the Parmesan is salty) and pepper to taste.

If possible, cover the bowl and refrigerate for a few hours, to give the quinoa flakes time to soak up any excess liquid so the mixture is slightly easier to handle. (This is not essential if you are short of time.)

Use 2 tablespoons to form dumplings, scraping the mixture off the one with the other, or roll a small scoop of mixture between your hands to make a neat little ball.

Once you are ready to cook the dumplings, use a bamboo steamer, colander or steamer insert in a saucepan with some shallow boiling water to steam them in batches, for about 10 minutes or until cooked through. You can brush some olive oil onto the insert to avoid the dumplings sticking to it.

Leave the dumplings to cool on a plate, covered, for a few minutes to firm them up, then serve with warmed Rich Tomato Sauce, a drizzle of good olive oil and grated Parmesan.

A little olive oil, butter, ghee or coconut oil

1 medium onion, diced

400g spinach, washed and roughly torn

120g can of sardines in olive oil, drained

1 teaspoon freshly grated nutmeg

2 garlic cloves, finely chopped

100g quinoa flakes (or fine oat flakes)

60g grated Parmesan cheese

1 egg white, lightly whisked

Sea salt and freshly ground black pepper

TO SERVE
1 quantity of Rich Tomato Sauce (page 153), warmed

Good olive oil

Grated Parmesan cheese

Millet and watercress sushi with creamy aduki bean paste

Few things give me more pleasure than homemade sushi. It is such a satisfactory process and allows for complete customisation, each roll providing a fresh canvas for the artist in the kitchen. If your first try looks a little messy, take heart – you will need only a few attempts to perfect your technique and, with all these deliciously nutritious ingredients, you won't mind practising. SERVES 4–6

For the paste, blend all the ingredients together in a blender or food processor until smooth, then set aside.

Toast the millet in a dry pan until it smells like popcorn. Add the water and salt and bring to the boil. Reduce the heat, cover and simmer, stirring occasionally, until soft and sticky, 25–30 minutes.

Meanwhile, whisk together the brown rice vinegar and honey. Pour the mixture over the cooked millet, spread it out on an oven tray and allow to cool just slightly; you want it still warm to assemble the rolls.

Place a nori sheet on a sushi mat, shiny side down and the ridges running parallel to the bamboo. Wet your fingertips and spread about 6 heaped tablespoons millet on the nori sheet, leaving a couple of centimetres free at the top and the bottom of the sheet. Use your fingertips to press the millet down on the nori very firmly. Millet does not have the same stickiness as rice, so you need to use some elbow grease here.

Spread 1 tablespoon bean paste over the lower half of the millet, then place a few pepper batons, some asparagus spears, 2 avocado strips and a few watercress sprigs on top.

Lift the bottom edge of your sushi mat and roll away from you, guiding the nori sheet downward and tucking it in around the filling to form a roll. Continue rolling the mat away from you until the nori is used up around the roll.

Turn the mat around and pull gently on the loose end while pressing the roll away from you to secure its shape. Use a very sharp knife to cut into 5 or 6 slices. Serve with the ginger, wasabi and shoyu dipping sauce.

NOTE:
Always try to buy naturally fermented soy sauce (shoyu), which is traditionally made by fermenting soybeans, water, wheat, and a special starter fungus. Because this can take up to a few years, many producers now cook the soybeans with hydrochloric acid, thereby eliminating the fermentation step, which is necessary in making soy digestible and beneficial.

6 nori sheets

1 red pepper (about 100g), cored and cut into 5cm batons

1 small bunch (100g) of slender asparagus stalks, trimmed and lightly steamed

1 avocado, peeled and cut into thin strips

1 small bunch of watercress, thick stems removed and leaves snipped

FOR THE PASTE
150g cooked aduki beans (50g uncooked, see page 152)

1½ tablespoons grated peeled ginger

1 tablespoon tahini

2 tablespoons lemon juice (about 1 lemon)

1 tablespoon maple syrup

Pinch of cayenne pepper

1 small garlic clove

Sea salt, to taste

FOR THE MILLET
300g millet, rinsed

750ml water

Large pinch of sea salt

60ml brown rice vinegar

1 tablespoon runny honey

TO SERVE
Naturally pickled ginger

Wasabi paste

Shoyu (or tamari) and rice vinegar dipping sauce (mixed together in a 2:1 ratio)

Barley and mustard greens risotto

Most people, myself included, love a good risotto – a creamy, unctuous dish that comfort-food dreams are made of. But what risotto boasts in yum factor, it lacks on the nutrition front. Here is a toothier version that will hopefully also satisfy those looking for a little more green in their lives. Remember to soak your barley for at least 8 hours before you plan to make this. Mustard greens and rocket are pungent and spicy leaves, so opt for spinach instead if you prefer a milder taste. Serve with extra grated or shaved Parmesan and a tomato salad. SERVES 2 (OR 4 AS A SIDE DISH OR STARTER)

Sauté the onion in some butter, ghee, olive oil or coconut oil with a pinch of sea salt over a medium heat until soft and translucent. Add the leeks and continue to cook until tender.

Turn up the heat and add the barley. Add a ladleful of stock at a time, stirring until it is completely absorbed before adding the next ladleful. Continue doing this until the barley is tender, for about 25–35 minutes, adding salt and pepper to taste along the way and stirring regularly. Remember that barley will never be soft and squidgy; even when cooked, the kernels remain chewy.

Spoon 2–3 tablespoons of the tender barley and the pulp of the Roasted Garlic into a blender (or tall container if using a stick blender), and add just enough hot stock (about 60ml) to be able to blend into a creamy paste. If it is too sticky or stodgy, add some more stock.

Now scrape the paste, which will help make the risotto creamy, back into the risotto pan, and stir in the mustard leaves, parsley, petits pois and Parmesan. Cover with a lid for a few minutes or until the leaves have wilted and the peas are cooked. Adjust the seasoning.

Turn off the heat and stir in the egg yolk. The residual heat from the barley will cook the yolk and make for a creamier end result. Scatter over some pea shoots and serve immediately.

1 medium onion, diced

Butter, ghee, or olive or coconut oil, for frying

2 medium leeks, halved lengthways and sliced into half-moons

220g pearl barley, soaked overnight, or for 8–12 hours, then rinsed

500–750ml fresh chicken or vegetable stock, kept just below simmering

1 quantity of Roasted Garlic (page 154)

1 bunch (about 50g) of mustard leaves, rocket or baby leaf spinach, roughly chopped

20g (small bunch) parsley, leaves only, finely chopped

110g fresh or frozen petits pois

50g grated Parmesan cheese, plus extra for serving

1 egg yolk, lightly whisked

Sea salt and freshly ground black pepper

Pea shoots, to serve (optional)

Grain-free cauliflower "pizza" with chard and olives

Thanks to popular diets such as the Paleo diet and other grain-free diets, we have come to love cauliflower for its versatility. Not only can it impersonate couscous, be turned into risotto and used instead of macaroni in mac 'n' cheese, it can also become a nutritious grain-free flour, by squeezing every last drop of liquid from it. SERVES 2

Preheat a pizza stone (or heavy, flat baking tray) in the oven at 220°C/430°F/Gas 7. Blitz the cauliflower in a food processor until it resembles couscous, then steam in a sieve or steamer over a small amount of simmering water until tender. Allow to cool completely.

Spoon the cauliflower into a nut milk bag or several layers of muslin and squeeze out all the liquid. You should end up with 200g cauliflower "flour". This process can seem laborious, but is essential.

In a bowl, combine the "flour" and the remaining ingredients for the base, with a pinch of salt and pepper, and mix well.

Using your hands, press the dough onto a large piece of oiled baking parchment, to about 5mm thick. Slide the baking parchment onto the hot pizza stone or baking tray in the oven and bake for 10 minutes. Remove from the oven, flip over and peel off the parchment. Return to the oven by sliding onto the pizza stone or baking sheet directly, then bake for another 5 minutes or until golden and crispy around the edges.

While the base is baking, gently cook the onion in a pan with some oil or ghee and a pinch of salt over a low heat. Once soft and translucent, turn up the heat to medium and add the tomatoes. When the tomatoes start to soften, add the garlic and cook for another 2–3 minutes. Add the chard and cook until wilted. Stir in the olives, remove from the heat and keep warm.

When the base is cooked, remove from the oven and allow to stand for a couple of minutes before topping with the chard mixture. Sprinkle on some crumbly cheese and chilli oil, if using.

NOTE:
The steamed cauliflower does take a long time to cool down, so if it's more convenient, prepare the "flour" in advance and keep refrigerated until ready to continue with the recipe.

FOR THE BASE

1 medium cauliflower, florets only

1 medium egg, lightly beaten

1 teaspoon dried mixed Italian herbs (oregano, marjoram, basil, etc.)

20g ground almonds

20g finely grated Parmesan cheese (optional)

Sea salt and freshly ground black pepper

FOR THE TOPPING

1 large red onion, cut in half through the core, peeled and sliced

Coconut oil, ghee or high-quality extra virgin olive oil

400g cherry tomatoes, halved

2 garlic cloves, pressed or mashed

200g chard, chopped into small bite-sized pieces (chop stalks separately if thick)

Large handful (about 50g) of pitted Kalamata olives

TO SERVE (OPTIONAL)
Crumbly goat's cheese

Chilli olive oil

Spring greens lasagne

As with most lasagne recipes, this one does take a little time, but it will feed a large crowd (or your family twice!) and it's a pleasure to know you have something ready to pop in the oven as soon as you get home from that long walk or exhausting shopping trip. The béchamel is made with butternut squash, so it comes out a lovely bright colour. SERVES 6

For the butternut béchamel, cook the butternut squash in a little water until tender. Drain and mash. You should end up with 350g mashed butternut squash.

Mix the arrowroot or kuzu with enough of the cold milk to dissolve it and form a thin paste. In a blender or with a stick blender, blend the rest of the milk with the mashed butternut mash until smooth.

Transfer the mixture to a small saucepan with the bay leaf and arrowroot or kuzu paste and heat, stirring continuously, until the mixture is simmering and starts to thicken. Cook for 1–2 minutes, then remove from the heat, generously season with salt and pepper and set aside. If the sauce is still too thin, add a little more kuzu or arrowroot dissolved in milk.

For the spring greens, heat some butter, or coconut or olive oil in a medium saucepan and sweat the onion with a pinch of salt. Add the spring greens and sauté until wilted. Remove from the heat and leave to cool. Meanwhile, preheat the oven to 180°C/350°F/Gas 4.

Put the ricotta, thyme leaves, eggs and sausage meat (or mushrooms) into a food processor and add the cold greens. Process until smooth.

To assemble, boil enough water to cover the base of a dish or shallow bowl that will fit 1 lasagna sheet. Steep the first lasagna sheet in the hot water for at least 10 seconds, or until it starts to soften. Remove and place in a medium ovenproof dish. Repeat until your first layer of sheets is complete. Break a sheet in half to fill any edges or corners if necessary.

Spread half the spring greens mixture over the lasagna, then half the Basic Tomato Sauce and half the butternut sauce. Repeat the process for the lasagna sheets with the second layer and repeat the layering of the sauces.

Top with the grated cheese, if using, and bake for 1 hour. Allow to stand for 10 minutes before serving, to give the lasagne a chance to firm up.

6–8 dried wholewheat or spinach lasagna sheets

1 quantity of Basic Tomato Sauce (page 153)

100g grated Gruyère cheese (optional)

FOR THE BUTTERNUT BÉCHAMEL
½ medium butternut squash, peeled, halved, deseeded and roughly chopped

2½ tablespoons arrowroot powder or crushed kuzu root starch, or 2 teaspoons cornflour

375ml milk of your choice (I use fresh almond milk)

1 bay leaf

Sea salt and freshly ground black pepper

FOR THE SPRING GREENS
Butter, or coconut or olive oil

1 medium onion, diced

2 heads of spring greens (about 600g), thick stalks removed, leaves roughly chopped

250g ricotta

1½ tablespoons thyme leaves

2 eggs, lightly beaten

400g sausage meat (from about 6 sausages) or 400g cooked mushrooms

Kale and lemon-stuffed chicken with cauliflower "couscous"

Nothing quite beats a roast chicken. This is an interesting version and even hard-nosed anti-veg campaigners have asked for second helpings. Although a staple in the "living foods" circles for the longest of times, raw cauliflower "couscous" has never been a favourite of mine. My tummy is a little sensitive and too many raw foods, especially of the cruciferous kind, tend to wreak havoc. However, I did not want to give up, which is how the recipe for this couscous came about. SERVES 6–8

Preheat the oven to 180°C/350°F/Gas 4.

Wash the kale, discarding any tough stalks, and put in a big saucepan with a little water. Cook over a medium heat until wilted, then transfer to a colander and leave to drain and cool before squeezing out any excess water.

Toast the cumin and coriander seeds in dry frying pan until fragrant. Grind in a spice grinder or with a pestle and mortar.

Put the kale, ground seeds, preserved lemon peel and salt into a food processor and process until finely ground. Stir through the goat's curd.

Put the chicken into a roasting tin. Gently slide your fingers between the skin and the flesh of the chicken to create pockets and fill these pockets with the kale mixture. I usually loosen the skin on the breasts and around the legs, pressing filling into all the nooks and crannies. That way you should be able to use it all up.

Put the cinnamon, garlic, lemon and onion quarters into the cavity of the chicken, cover the roasting tin with foil and roast for 35 minutes. Remove the foil and roast for a further 35–45 minutes, or until the juices run clear when the thickest part of a thigh is pricked with a skewer. Allow to rest, covered, for at least 10 minutes.

While the chicken is roasting, blitz the cauliflower in a food processor until it resembles couscous. Stir-fry the cauliflower couscous in a medium–hot pan with a little butter or oil until tender, 5–8 minutes..

Mix the cooked cauliflower in a serving bowl with the remaining couscous ingredients, except the flaked almonds, then sprinkle flaked almonds on top and serve with the chicken.

PHOTOGRAPH ON PAGES 96–97

200g kale

1 teaspoon cumin seeds

1 teaspoon coriander seeds

1 medium preserved lemon (40–50g), flesh removed and peel finely chopped

1 scant teaspoon sea salt

150g goat's curd or rindless soft goat's cheese

1 large chicken (about 2kg), giblets removed

1 cinnamon stick

2 garlic cloves, peeled and crushed

1 lemon, washed and pricked with a skewer in several places, then quartered lengthways

1 medium onion, peeled and quartered

FOR THE CAULIFLOWER "COUSCOUS"
1 large cauliflower (600–700g), trimmed and separated into florets

1 small red onion, finely chopped and soaked in cold water for 15 minutes

70g (about 10) preservative-free dried apricots, diced

1 teaspoon ras-el-hanout (see page 155 to make your own)

2cm piece of fresh turmeric root, grated (or ½ teaspoon ground)

Knob of butter (optional)

2 tablespoons extra virgin olive oil

Juice of 1 lemon

Pinch of sea salt

50g flaked almonds, toasted

Broccoli and brown rice bake
with soft-boiled eggs

*The success of this dish rests on using the most flavoursome stock.
If you are not vegetarian, I would recommend chicken stock,
otherwise be sure to use a veggie stock with a deep flavour. If
you have any leftovers, add to 1–2 whisked eggs and stir in 1–2
tablespoons flour to make little fritters.* SERVES 4 (OR 6 AS A SIDE DISH)

Preheat the oven to 180°C/350°F/Gas 4.

Put all the ingredients, except the broccoli and chives, into a
medium ovenproof dish or casserole that has a lid, and stir to
combine. Cover and bake in the oven for 45–50 minutes.

Meanwhile, cut the large and smaller stalks of the broccoli into
small dice and separate the florets into small bits.

Carefully remove the dish from the oven, add the broccoli stems
and give the contents a good stir. Cover and return to the oven.
After 10 minutes, add the florets, give it another stir, ensuring
the top layer of rice is mixed under, and bake for a further
5–10 minutes.

Remove from the oven and test the rice; it should be tender and
sticky, almost like risotto. If it is still a little *al dente*, return to the
oven for another 5 minutes.

Remove from the oven and leave to stand, covered, for 10
minutes before sprinkling with the chives and serving with soft-
boiled eggs and a grating of Parmesan, if you like.

680ml hot vegetable or chicken stock

1 large onion, chopped into small dice

2 garlic cloves, finely chopped

1 tablespoon extra virgin olive oil

1 heaped teaspoon sea salt

1 heaped teaspoon mixed dried
herbes de Provence

1 teaspoon ground turmeric

1 teaspoon ground paprika

1 teaspoon ground coriander

60g (about 10 halves) sun-dried
tomatoes in olive oil, cut into thin strips

300g short-grain brown rice, rinsed

1 small head (300–320g) of broccoli

Handful of chives, finely chopped

TO SERVE
Soft-boiled eggs

Freshly grated Parmesan cheese
(optional)

Chickpea and chard pancakes with aubergine stew

Another favourite in our household, chickpea pancakes work well with many toppings and flavours. Timing is important, as the batter needs to stand for at least a few hours before cooking the pancakes, and the pan needs to be preheated. They are also best served while they are still hot and crispy, so we usually eat them in shifts. SERVES 4

To make the pancake batter, put the gram flour in a bowl, make a well in the centre and whisk in the coconut oil, a large pinch of salt and most of the water until you have a thick batter. Add more water if necessary, then set aside for 4 hours.

Preheat the oven to 220°C/430°F/Gas 7.

Heat the olive oil in a saucepan and sauté the onion for the batter with a pinch of salt over a medium heat until soft and translucent. Add the rosemary and fry for another minute before scraping into a food processor and setting aside.

Tip the chard stalks into the pan, add a tiny bit of water, cover and "steam" until tender. Add the chard leaves and cook, uncovered, until wilted, for about 1 minute or longer if the leaves are very coarse, and the saucepan is dry.

Add this mixture to the food processor (no need to squeeze it out first), process until very fine and set aside. Stir into the chickpea batter just before you cook the pancakes.

For the aubergine stew, heat some fat of your choice in a saucepan and sauté the red onion with a pinch of salt for a few minutes. Add the garlic and aubergine and increase the heat a little. As soon as the aubergine is halfway to being tender, add the chopped tomatoes, thyme leaves, chopped pepper and cayenne pepper, cover and cook, stirring occasionally for 20–30 minutes until the aubergine is soft but not squishy.

Add the orange juice and parsley, simmer for another minute, season, remove from the heat and keep warm.

Meanwhile, place one large or two smaller cast-iron skillets or heavy-based stainless steel pans in the oven with a large knob of ghee or coconut oil. As soon as it is very hot (but not smoking) and the fat covers the base in a noticeable layer, remove from the oven and ladle enough of the chickpea mixture into the pan(s) to make several small, or one large pancake. You will hear a sizzling sound. Slide back into the oven and bake for 10–20 minutes or until very crispy around the edges and slightly golden on top. Repeat with the remaining pancake mixture until it is all used up.

Serve straight from the oven with the aubergine stew and Greek yoghurt or Vegan Greek-style "Yoghurt".

FOR THE PANCAKES

240g gram flour (chickpea flour)

20ml (1½ tablespoons) liquid coconut oil

310ml tepid water

A little olive oil

1 medium onion, chopped

1 heaped tablespoon finely chopped rosemary

200g chard, thick stalks cut out and finely chopped, leaves torn into smaller pieces

Ghee or coconut oil, for frying

Sea salt

FOR THE AUBERGINE STEW

Coconut oil, butter or extra virgin olive oil

1 large red onion, finely chopped

2 garlic cloves, finely chopped

480–500g (about 2 medium) aubergines, cut into 1.5cm dice

480–500g (about 5) large tomatoes, blanched, skinned, fibrous core removed, chopped

1 heaped tablespoon thyme leaves, finely chopped

1 orange pepper, cut into small dice

Pinch of cayenne pepper

40ml freshly squeezed orange juice (about 1 medium orange)

25g (1 small bunch) flat-leaf parsley, finely chopped

Greek yoghurt or Vegan Greek-style "Yoghurt" (page 157), to serve

Lentil, pak choy and mushroom curry

This is one of my favourite mid-week suppers. I often increase the quantity of pak choy, as I love the taste and the shocks of green. It can be made ahead and kept in the fridge for a few days, but I would reserve the pak choy leaves, coriander and ginger juice to be added to the heated curry just before serving. SERVES 3–4

Preheat the oven to 180°C/350°F/Gas 4.

Toss the butternut dice in some salt, pepper and oil, then roast in the oven for 40–50 minutes until tender and golden, turning the pieces over using a spatula after about 20 minutes.

Meanwhile, heat a little oil in a large pan, add the onion and sauté until soft and translucent. Add the garlic and cook for another couple of minutes, then tip into a small bowl. Heat a little more oil, add the mushrooms and fry, in batches, over a medium-high heat until nicely browned and tender.

Add the lentils, chilli flakes, coconut milk and stock, and simmer, uncovered, for about 15 minutes until the lentils are almost tender. Add the pak choy stems, increase the heat to high and cook for another 5 minutes, or until the sauce has thickened and is sticky around the edges of the pan.

Add the pak choy leaves and, as soon as they have wilted, add the ginger juice to taste, and the coriander. Top with the roasted squash and serve immediately, either as it is, or with cauliflower "couscous" or brown basmati rice cooked with sliced ginger, ground turmeric and cloves.

1 large butternut squash, peeled, halved, seeds removed, and flesh chopped into large dice

Grapeseed, coconut, macadamia or other oil

1 large onion, finely diced

3 medium garlic cloves, finely chopped

1 punnet (120–130g) oyster mushrooms, cleaned and cut into bite-sized pieces

1 punnet (120–130g) shiitake mushrooms, cleaned, stalks removed and thickly sliced

100g Puy lentils, soaked overnight, then rinsed

Large pinch of dried chilli flakes, or to taste

400ml can of coconut milk

125ml vegetable stock

200g pak choy, stems thickly sliced and leaves roughly chopped

Juice from a thumb-sized piece of ginger, grated and juice squeezed out (use a nut milk bag, muslin cloth or your hands)

Large handful (40–50g) of coriander, finely chopped

Sea salt and freshly ground black pepper

Cape Malay-style mutton curry

South African cuisine is a wonderful mishmash of cultural influences and the ready access to tasty fresh produce in most parts of the country is a cook's dream. A personal highlight is the Cape Malay heritage with its richly flavoured and Indonesian-inspired dishes. If you are vegetarian, replace the meat with chickpeas and roasted pumpkin or butternut squash. This recipe does make quite a lot, but it seems a waste to make a smaller portion if you are going to go to all the effort. Any leftovers can be frozen. SERVES 6–8

Grind the fennel and coriander seeds, chilli flakes, peppercorns, cardamom and cumin seeds in a mortar and pestle (or use a spice grinder) until finely ground.

Heat some oil in a shallow pan, large enough to fit all the pieces of meat, and brown the meat on all sides. Remove from the pan and set aside.

In the same pan, sweat the onion until soft and translucent. Add the ginger and cook for another few minutes. Add the ground spices, turmeric, garam masala, cinnamon stick, cloves and bay leaves, and stir for a couple of minutes. Stir in the remaining ingredients except the spinach and pineapple, and tuck the pieces of meat into the sauce.

Cover and simmer for at least 2 hours, or until the meat is very tender, gently turning over the pieces of meat once or twice during cooking.

When the meat is close to falling off the bone, skim off excess fat, carefully transfer the meat to a serving dish and check the sauce for any small bones that may have fallen off during cooking. Stir the spinach and pineapple into the sauce and simmer, covered, for a further 10 minutes, or until the spinach is wilted and the pineapple is cooked.

Serve the meat on turmeric rice with the sauce, topped with banana slices and desiccated coconut.

NOTE:
The curry's flavours develop over time, so leave it in the fridge for a day or two before serving, if you can, and enjoy the thought of having another meal ready for later that same week.

3 teaspoons fennel seeds

1½ teaspoons coriander seeds

1–2 teaspoons dried chilli flakes, to taste

½ teaspoon black peppercorns

Seeds of 10 cardamom pods

2 teaspoons cumin seeds

Grapeseed or coconut oil, for frying

1.2kg mutton (or lamb) neck pieces, bone in

1 large onion (200–220g), finely chopped

1 tablespoon grated peeled ginger

2 teaspoons ground turmeric (or 3 teaspoons freshly grated root)

1 tablespoon garam masala

1 cinnamon stick

4 cloves

2 bay leaves

2 teaspoons sea salt

2 x 400g cans of chopped tomatoes

2 tablespoons tomato purée

2–3 garlic cloves, finely chopped

2 teaspoons brown sugar

2 tablespoons cider vinegar

200–250g baby leaf spinach

1 small pineapple, flesh cut into small cubes

TO SERVE
Turmeric rice

2 ripe but firm medium bananas, sliced

Desiccated coconut

Brussels sprout, leek and potato cake

This is a delicious way to prepare a bunch of humble vegetables. Serve with sour cream or Greek yoghurt, sustainably sourced caviar (try Mottra caviar) and smoked wild salmon, for a festive occasion, or with roasted tomatoes and a large mixed salad for lunch or a light supper. It is also terrific as a brunch dish with wilted spinach and poached eggs. SERVES 4–6

Preheat the oven to 180°C/350°F/Gas 4.

Use a small knife to cut a cross into each potato (or prick a few times with a fork) and roast for 1–1½ hours, or until just tender. As soon as they are cool enough to handle, scoop out the insides and mash with a fork, leaving them very lumpy. Increase the oven temperature to 220°C/430°F/Gas 7.

While the potatoes are baking, heat a third of the butter in a medium (about 24cm) ovenproof frying pan and fry the sage for a minute or two. Add the leek and a large pinch of salt, and cook over a medium heat until tender. Scrape into a large bowl and set aside.

Increase the heat in the pan, add half the remaining butter, shake off any excess water from the sprouts and sauté until nicely browned. Scrape into the bowl with the leeks. Add the crushed potatoes to the bowl with some salt, pepper and the mustard, and mix well.

Heat the remaining butter in the pan and, once it is very hot, spoon in the potato mixture (you should hear it sizzle) and press it down with the back of a large spoon until it is smooth and compact. Transfer to the oven and bake for 30 minutes, or until the edges and top are golden brown (cover with foil for the last few minutes if it gets too dark on top).

Remove from the oven and allow to cool for at least 5 minutes, before using a spatula to loosen the cake around the edges and, if possible, along the base. Place a plate on top and flip it over to release the cake. Slice and serve.

3 medium (850–900g total) baking potatoes

30g butter

3 heaped tablespoons finely shredded sage

1 medium leek (about 150g), trimmed slightly, halved lengthways and thinly sliced

200g Brussels sprouts, trimmed, quartered (or halved if using baby sprouts) and steamed until just tender

1 tablespoon wholegrain mustard

Sea salt and freshly ground black pepper

Salad
greens

Warm black rice noodle salad

This is a subtle, comforting dish, best served still slightly warm. If you are having this as a main course, add some cooked mung beans or other protein of your choice and perhaps a few halved cherry tomatoes for colour. If you cannot find black rice noodles (which provide a great colour contrast), regular soba or rice noodles will do just fine. SERVES 4 AS A SIDE DISH

Cook the rice noodles until *al dente*, according to the packet instructions, then drain, rinse well and transfer to a large mixing bowl. Toss to coat with a little untoasted sesame or olive oil (to prevent the noodles from sticking together) and a pinch of salt, and set aside.

Heat the rapeseed oil in a pan and fry the shallot with a pinch of salt over a medium-high heat for a few minutes or until soft, stirring regularly to avoid burning (some browning is fine).

Add the garlic and five-spice powder and cook for another couple of minutes before adding the pak choy stems. At this point you may want to add some water to deglaze the pan and help the pak choy cook, but make sure you cook the pan dry before adding the leaves.

When the stems are tender, add the leaves and cook until just wilted, for about 30 seconds. Scrape into the bowl with the noodles, then add the remaining salad ingredients to the bowl.

Combine all the dressing ingredients, with salt to taste, in a jar, screw on the lid and give it a good shake. Taste and adjust the seasoning if necessary – the dressing should taste very intense, as its flavour is diluted once added to the salad. Dress the salad and gently toss to coat.

80g black rice noodles

Untoasted (virgin) sesame oil, or extra virgin olive oil

1 teaspoon rapeseed oil, or other neutral-tasting cooking oil

1 echalion (banana) shallot (60–70g), chopped into small dice

2 large garlic cloves, finely chopped

1 teaspoon Chinese five-spice powder (see page 155 to make your own)

300g pak choy or tatsoi, stalks finely chopped and leaves torn into smaller pieces (or left whole if small)

100g double-podded broad beans (see page 66), or peas (fresh or frozen)

1–2 spring onions, white and green part, finely sliced on the diagonal

80g (small handful) mange tout, trimmed and any strings removed

1 thin yellow or green courgette (80–100g), finely sliced on the diagonal using a mandolin or vegetable swivel peeler

Sea salt

FOR THE DRESSING

1 tablespoon finely chopped shallot

1 garlic clove, finely chopped

3 tablespoons untoasted (virgin) sesame oil

1½ tablespoons brown (or regular) rice vinegar

½ teaspoon wasabi powder or paste, or to taste

1–1½ tablespoons tamari or shoyu

Lettuce cups with sticky brown rice and vegetable crudités

I love meals that invite involvement from diners. It allows them to let their hair down, get their hands dirty and tailor-make each bite to suit their taste. The dressing and sauce for the rice can be made in advance, and the prepared crudités will keep well for a few hours in an airtight container in the fridge. SERVES 4

Combine all the ingredients for the dressing in a small bowl and set aside. Prepare the Sticky Brown Rice following the method on page 156.

While the rice is cooking, put the coconut flesh and water, ginger, garlic, chilli, lime zest and juice, oil, fish sauce and a pinch of salt in a blender, and process to a relatively smooth sauce.

Heat the rapeseed oil in a pan and sauté the spring onions with a pinch of salt for a minute or so.

Stir into the sticky rice with the coconut sauce, as soon as the rice is cooked.

Give each guest a head or two of lettuce and a plate, then place the dressing, sticky rice, vegetables and chicken/tofu in the centre of the table and enjoy watching your guests fill each lettuce leaf to their own taste.

FOR THE DRESSING
15g (very small handful) coriander, finely chopped

½ teaspoon shoyu or tamari

½ teaspoon fish sauce (optional)

1 tablespoon rice vinegar

½–1 tablespoon palm sugar (or dark muscovado sugar)

1 teaspoon grated peeled ginger

Juice of 1 lime (1½–2 tablespoons)

1 tablespoon untoasted (virgin) sesame oil

1 teaspoon sesame seeds

FOR THE STICKY RICE
1 quantity of hot Sticky Brown Rice (page 156)

30g fresh coconut flesh (the mature meat, sold cubed in supermarkets)

2 tablespoons coconut water, preferably unpasteurised

1 teaspoon grated peeled ginger

1 medium garlic clove, finely chopped

½–1 red Thai chilli, finely chopped (seeds and/or membranes removed if you prefer it less spicy)

Grated zest and juice (1–1½ tablespoons) of 1 small lime

2 tablespoons avocado oil, or untoasted (virgin) sesame oil

½–1 teaspoon fish sauce, to taste

1 teaspoon rapeseed oil

4 spring onions, thinly sliced, plus extra to serve

Sea salt

TO SERVE
4 or more baby cos or Little Gem lettuces, trimmed

1 medium carrot, cut into matchsticks

70g sugar snap or snow peas, trimmed, any strings removed, cut into matchsticks

¼ large cucumber, cut into matchsticks

Shredded, cooked chicken, fried tofu, or sliced, cooked beef fillet (optional)

Kohlrabi and pickled onion salad

When all you crave on a bleak, lazy or stressful day is something crunchy and cheeky, yet deeply satisfying, make this salad. Kohlrabi, either the whitish-green or purple-skinned variety, is not often available at regular supermarkets, but most local and ethnic grocers stock them. Cucumbers are notorious for drawing water, so leave it to drain for as long as possible and only dress the salad just before serving. SERVES 4 AS A SIDE DISH

For the dressing, mix the grated cucumber with the salt and leave to drain in a colander set over a plate or bowl.

Mix together the remaining dressing ingredients and set aside.

For the pickled onion, whisk all the ingredients except the onion in a small bowl until the sugar and salt have dissolved. Add the onion slices and ensure everything is covered with the liquid. Set aside for about 1 hour, or until the onion has turned bright pink. Drain, removing the juniper berries.

For the salad, toss the kohlrabi, carrot, basil and pickled onion with the dressing and arrange on a serving plate. Scatter over the cress and tuck in right away.

FOR THE DRESSING

½ medium cucumber, peeled, halved lengthways, deseeded (using an apple corer or teaspoon) and coarsely grated

Large pinch of sea salt

2 tablespoons mayonnaise (see page 154 to make your own, but omit the tarragon)

1 tablespoon lemon juice
(about ½ lemon)

2 tablespoons extra virgin olive oil

Pinch of unrefined brown sugar

1 tablespoon finely chopped chives

FOR THE PICKLED ONION

1 tablespoon coarse sea salt

1 tablespoon unrefined brown sugar

125ml cider vinegar

5 juniper berries, lightly bashed but left whole

5 peppercorns, crushed

1 medium red onion, cut in half through the core, peeled and thinly sliced

FOR THE SALAD

1 kohlrabi (350–400g), peeled and julienned

1 medium carrot, coarsely grated

Handful of basil leaves, torn into smaller pieces

2 large handfuls of cress

Raw bitters salad

This immensely health-supportive salad is very tasty, as well as being lovely to look at. Most bitter foods are not only very nutrient dense but also help to absorb those nutrients, as they stimulate the production of gastric acid in the stomach. The better your food is digested, the more nutrients you will absorb from your food. Bitters balance your taste buds and control sweet cravings, while also boosting your metabolism and fighting free radicals. Serve with Macadamia Nut Spread (see page 157) when you need a little more substance. SERVES 4–6

1 small radicchio, leaves torn

50–70g wild or regular rocket

2 purple or white chicory, leaves torn

1 red grapefruit, peeled and segmented

1 pink grapefruit, peeled and segmented

Large handful of mange tout, trimmed

110g freshly shelled petits pois or garden peas, or frozen peas blanched in boiling water for 10 seconds and refreshed in ice-cold water

2 large avocados, sliced or diced

75g mixed sunflower and pumpkin seeds

Large handful of basil leaves, finely shredded (see Note on page 40)

FOR THE DRESSING
1 teaspoon light miso paste, preferably unpasteurised

80ml cider vinegar, preferably unpasteurised

½–1 tablespoon maple syrup

1 teaspoon Dijon mustard

250ml extra virgin olive oil

1 tablespoon finely chopped shallots or red onion

50g (1 bunch) parsley, finely chopped

Sea salt and freshly ground black pepper

Toss all the salad ingredients together in a bowl.

For the dressing, whisk together the miso paste, vinegar, maple syrup, mustard and some salt and pepper. While whisking, add the olive oil in a thin but steady stream, until emulsified. Stir in the shallots and parsley, then toss through the salad.

Rainbow slaw

Every cook should have a good coleslaw recipe in their repertoire. This one is particularly refreshing and tantalising, and the dressing takes it out of the sphere of the ordinary. SERVES 4–6

½ large pineapple, peeled and "eyes" removed

½ small red cabbage (about 250g), finely shredded

½ Chinese cabbage (about 250g), finely shredded

350g carrots, coarsely grated

1 small romaine lettuce head, halved lengthways and finely shredded

25g (1 bunch) chives

20 large mint leaves, finely shredded (see Note on page 40)

2 red chillies, very finely chopped

Handful of dry-roasted peanuts (or other nuts)

FOR THE DRESSING
2 teaspoons shoyu or tamari

2 tablespoons cider vinegar

1 heaped tablespoon grated peeled ginger

1 tablespoon untoasted (virgin) sesame oil

1 tablespoon toasted sesame oil

2 tablespoons unsalted peanut (or other nut) butter

1 teaspoon raw honey

½ teaspoon sea salt

For the dressing, put all the ingredients in a glass jar, screw on the lid and shake vigorously. Set aside.

Grate the pineapple on the coarse side of a box grater. I usually do this on a tray, as it does get messy. Scoop the pineapple flesh into a colander or sieve, set it over a bowl and leave to drain.

Put the shredded cabbages, carrots and lettuce into a large mixing bowl. Snip the bunch of chives into tiny pieces straight into the bowl using scissors. Add the mint and chillies.

Add the drained pineapple to the salad with enough dressing to coat. Give it a good mix and serve with the peanuts sprinkled on top.

Spiced grain and kale salad

This is a virtuous salad that manages to fill you up and taste great. If you don't have ready-cooked portions of grains and lentils in the freezer (which makes this salad a whole lot easier to prepare), follow the instructions in the Note below. Use double quantities of quinoa, instead of the barley, if you are avoiding gluten. And feel free to use whole spices and grind them yourself. SERVES 4

Heat the butter in a medium pan, add the onions and sauté over a gentle heat until they start to soften. Increase the heat to medium and cook, stirring regularly, until they start to caramelise, for about 30 minutes.

Meanwhile, put the kale into a big mixing bowl, add the salt, lemon juice and olive oil, then massage the leaves with your fingertips for a few minutes, until they become soft and silky. Add the remaining salad ingredients and set aside.

For the dressing, toast the spices in a dry frying pan over a medium heat until they become fragrant. Transfer to a jar with the rest of the dressing ingredients, with salt and pepper, to taste, screw the lid on tightly and give a vigorous shake. Pour the dressing over the salad and toss to coat.

NOTE:
To cook the grains and lentils from scratch, soak about 45g each of the quinoa, barley, basmati rice and lentils separately in plenty of water overnight, then rinse each separately and start by bringing the barley and a large pinch of salt to the boil in four times its volume of fresh water. After 10 minutes (or 20 if you are using pot barley), add the lentils and rice, and after another 15 minutes or so, the quinoa. Cook for a further 5–10 minutes or until all the grains and lentils are tender, then remove from the heat. Strain off any water, return the mixture to the pan and cover with a lid for a further 5 minutes.

Knob of butter

2 large onions, cut in half through the core, peeled and sliced

100g kale, tough stalks removed, chopped

Pinch of sea salt

½ tablespoon lemon juice

½ tablespoon extra virgin olive oil

400g mixture of cooked quinoa, pearl (or pot) barley, brown basmati rice and Puy lentils

35g raisins and/or dried cherries

70g shelled, unroasted hazelnuts, roughly chopped

20g (1 small bunch) dill, largest stalks removed, finely chopped

FOR THE DRESSING
¼ teaspoon ground cloves

½ teaspoon freshly grated nutmeg

1½ teaspoons ground cumin

1½ teaspoons ground coriander

1½ teaspoons ground fennel seeds

2 tablespoons extra virgin olive oil

Grated zest of 1 lemon

80–125ml kefir or stirred natural yoghurt

1–2 teaspoons sea salt

Freshly ground black pepper

Sea vegetable salad

This is a great salad to introduce people to sea vegetables. The mix of sea vegetables can include arame (with a mild sweetness and chewy texture), hijiki (bolder and with a subtle anise flavour), and dulse (with an earthy taste). All sea veg need to be rehydrated by soaking in room-temperature water just until pliable (10 minutes for arame and dulse, 20 minutes for hiziki), then drained and squeezed. Most supermarkets (and healthfood stores) sell sea veg in the Asian sections. SERVES 4 (OR 6 AS A SIDE DISH)

Handful of mixed sea vegetables, rehydrated according to the packet instructions, and finely chopped if large

2 medium red and/or golden beetroot, peeled and cut into matchsticks

1 watermelon radish (about 130g), cut into matchsticks

2 celery stalks, cut into thirds and then into matchsticks

1 large cucumber (330–350g), peeled, halved lengthways, deseeded (use an apple corer or teaspoon) and sliced into thin half-moons

250g seedless red grapes, halved

Few handfuls of shredded red or white chicory, baby rocket or lamb's lettuce (mâche) (optional)

FOR THE DRESSING
2 tablespoons lemon juice (about 1 small lemon)

1 medium garlic clove, peeled

1½ teaspoons honey

80ml extra virgin olive oil

2½ tablespoons light miso paste

1 heaped teaspoon grated peeled ginger

2 thin spring onions, or 1 thick, green part thinly sliced and reserved for the salad, white part roughly chopped

For the dressing, blend all the ingredients, except the green onion slices, in a blender until creamy.

Combine the salad ingredients, including the green onion slices, and toss with enough dressing to coat.

Serve with the Watercress Oat Cakes (page 136) and the Smoked Mackerel and Watercress Mousse (page 52), or warm falafels.

PHOTOGRAPH ON PAGE 53

Lamb's lettuce, pumpkin seed and apple salad

This is definitely a green salad, with the soft and silky lamb's lettuce, crunchy Gems and sweet-sour apples. The pumpkin seed oil does add a lovely flavour, and is a fantastic ingredient to have in your storecupboard, but feel free to use avocado oil or just olive oil instead. You will most likely have some leftover dressing, but it keeps well in the fridge for a few days and can be enjoyed with any salad or shredded vegetables. If you are preparing the salad in advance, do not dress it until just before serving and toss the apple slices in some lemon juice diluted with water to prevent browning. SERVES 4–6

100g lamb's lettuce (mâche)

2 Little Gem lettuces, leaves separated

2 green apples, cored, halved and sliced

150g sugar snap peas, any strings removed

80g pumpkin seeds, toasted in a dry frying pan until they start to pop

FOR THE DRESSING
1 small or ½ large ripe avocado

80ml lemon juice (2–3 lemons)

1–1½ tablespoons maple syrup or honey, to taste

125ml mixture of pumpkin seed oil and olive oil (1:3 ratio), or all olive oil

1 teaspoon Dijon mustard

30g (small handful) fresh coriander, thickest stems removed

Put all the salad ingredients, except the pumpkin seeds, into a large bowl.

In a blender, blend together the ingredients for the dressing and pour enough over the salad to coat lightly and evenly, when gently tossed.

Sprinkle with the toasted pumpkin seeds and serve immediately.

Herb salad

This is a wonderfully refreshing green salad that is delicious with a rich or heavy main course, or served as a first course to awaken the palate. I sometimes add a finely shredded chicory or a tomato. Use up all the dressing – the salad needs it. If you don't like the sharp taste of raw onion, soak it in cold water for 15 minutes after chopping, then drain. SERVES 4

1–2 pitta breads, cut into very thin strips

1 head romaine lettuce, coarsely chopped

25–30g (1 small bunch) flat-leaf parsley, leaves only, finely chopped

15g (3–4 sprigs) basil, leaves only, torn into bite-sized pieces

10g (½ small bunch) dill, thickest part of stalks discarded, roughly chopped

15g (½ bunch) chives, snipped into small pieces

2–3 mint sprigs, leaves only, finely shredded

10g (1 handful) tarragon sprigs, leaves only, roughly chopped

FOR THE DRESSING
1 tablespoon finely chopped red onion

½ teaspoon dried oregano

1 tablespoon finely chopped fresh thyme leaves

3–4 oregano sprigs, leaves only (about 2 heaped tablespoons), finely chopped (or use a little more dried if you can't find fresh)

1 tablespoon red wine vinegar

3 tablespoons extra virgin olive oil

Large pinch of unrefined brown sugar

Large pinch of sea salt

Preheat the oven to 180°C/350°F/Gas 4.

Spread the strips of pitta out on a baking tray in a single layer and bake in the oven for 20–25 minutes until crunchy.

For the dressing, put all the ingredients in a glass jar, screw the lid on tightly and shake vigorously until the sugar has dissolved.

Toss the salad ingredients and pitta chips together. Dress the salad and serve immediately.

Lentil and spinach salad

Hearty, moreish, and a staple on my weekly menu, the secret to this dish is a delicious aged balsamic vinegar and lovely ripe avocados. Add a cup of cooked brown rice to turn it into a filling lunch option. Make a batch of the slow-roasted tomatoes and enjoy them on toast, with scrambled eggs or blended into soups and sauces throughout the week. SERVES 2–4

150g baby leaf spinach

350g cooked black (or "beluga") or Puy lentils (see page 152)

150g goat's milk feta cheese, crumbled

4–5 artichoke hearts (about 60g) in oil, drained and quartered

3 spring onions, green and white part, trimmed and thinly sliced

100–125g Slow-roasted Cherry Tomatoes (page 154)

2 ripe avocados, cut into medium dice

FOR THE DRESSING
½ tablespoon aged balsamic vinegar

½ teaspoon Dijon mustard

Smidgen of honey or maple syrup, to taste

60ml extra virgin olive oil

Sea salt and freshly ground black pepper

Toss all the salad ingredients together, reserving some feta and spring onion slices to decorate.

For the dressing, put all the ingredients, with salt and pepper to taste, in a jar, screw on the lid and shake vigorously until emulsified. Dress the salad and toss gently just before serving.

The love salad

So-called because it's perfect for a romantic, celebratory dinner, this salad is a satisfying meal and quite beautiful to look at. You do need to start on it the night before, though, as both the cheese and duck need some time. Omit the duck if you prefer a vegetarian salad. SERVES 4

Score the duck skin in a criss-cross pattern using a very sharp knife, being careful not to cut into the meat. Whisk the balsamic vinegar, honey, oil and lemon juice together in a bowl large enough to fit the duck snugly, then add the garlic and rosemary. Add the duck breasts to the marinade, coating them well, then marinate, skin side up, in the fridge for at least 12 hours.

For the salad, line a sieve with a few layers of muslin and scoop the yoghurt into the centre. Place the sieve in a bowl, cover with a clean tea towel and leave to strain in the fridge overnight.

The next day, preheat the oven to 160°C/320°F/Gas 3. Cut the beetroot into thin slices, 2mm thick, using a mandolin, and reserve any offcuts in a small bowl. Toss the beetroot slices with the olive oil and a little salt, transfer to a baking tray and bake for 35–45 minutes, removing any slices that have browned sooner, as they will taste bitter if too dark. Set aside to cool and turn crisp.

While the beetroot is roasting, remove the duck breast from the marinade, reserving the marinade, pat them dry and place skin side down in a heavy, preferably cast-iron, frying pan. Cook over a low to medium heat for 10–12 minutes, until the skin is crisp and brown. Do not try to rush this step, as the low temperature will help render the fat in the skin. Turn the duck over and cook for a further 2 minutes, then remove from the pan.

Use kitchen paper to wipe the pan clean, turn the heat up to high, return the duck to the pan skin side up and pour in the reserved marinade. Simmer for less than a minute, to reduce the marinade, then remove the pan from the heat, cover and keep warm for at least 10 minutes. The residual heat will finish cooking the duck.

While the duck is resting, scoop the goat's curd from the muslin-lined sieve and transfer to a bowl. Season with salt and pepper and stir in just enough of the beetroot juice that will have collected in the bowl of offcuts to colour the cheese a lovely pink.

For the dressing, put all the ingredients in a glass jar, screw the lid on tightly and shake until the honey has dissolved.

Put the greens, berries and radishes in a dish. Slice the duck breasts and add, along with the dressing, then toss to coat. Pile the beetroot slices on top and dollop the fresh curd to the side.

2 duck breasts, skin on

3 tablespoons balsamic vinegar

1 tablespoon honey

3 tablespoons extra virgin olive oil

Juice of ½ lemon

2 large garlic cloves, peeled and bashed with the flat side of a large knife

2 rosemary sprigs

FOR THE SALAD

200g full-cream thick goat's milk yoghurt

500g raw beetroot, peeled

1½ tablespoons extra virgin olive oil

100g mixture of beetroot greens (finely shredded if not young and tender), radish greens and baby ruby chard

200g strawberries

100g raspberries

5 large red and/or purple radishes, very thinly sliced using a mandolin

Sea salt and freshly ground black pepper

FOR THE DRESSING

3 tablespoons extra virgin olive oil

1 tablespoon raspberry vinegar (or crush a few raspberries and mix with 1 tablespoon apple cider vinegar)

1 teaspoon honey

1 teaspoon each of black and white poppy seeds (or black only, if white is hard to find)

¼ teaspoon cayenne pepper

The super salad

The term "superfood" has lost its gloss, having been overused by gym bunnies and abused by marketeers in the food industry. But some foods are most definitely big hitters in the nutrient department and are the opposite of empty calories. Here is a salad that makes use of some of these delicious, naturally potent foods that leave you feeling nourished, not duped. Soaking the quinoa overnight prior to cooking will improve its nutritional value and make it more digestible. SERVES 4

Preheat the oven to 160°C/320°F/Gas 3.

Wash the broccoli and dry well by shaking off any excess water. Trim, but leave some of the stem intact, then separate into similar-sized florets, cutting through the stem lengthways to give each floret a little handle.

Toss the broccoli with the oil and a little salt, spread out on a baking tray and roast in the oven for 20–25 minutes, or until just tender, with a delicious crunch and caramelised around the edges. Do not let it get too dark, or it will taste bitter.

If you prefer toasted nuts, toast the walnuts on a baking tray in the oven at the same time as you are roasting the broccoli, for about 10–15 minutes, or until crunchy. Allow to cool, then roughly chop. If not toasting, just roughly chop.

For the dressing, put all the ingredients in a glass jar, screw the lid on tightly and give it a good shake.

Toss all the ingredients for the salad together, except the hemp seeds. Add the dressing, toss to coat and sprinkle over the hemp seeds to serve.

NOTE:
An easy way to remove the pomegranate seeds is to cut the fruit in half then, holding one half over a large bowl with the cut side facing down, knock the tough outer peel with the back of a large metal spoon until the seeds pop out.

350g (2 small to medium heads) broccoli

1–2 tablespoons chilli oil or regular olive oil

60g shelled, unroasted walnuts

Large handful of salad sprouts of your choice (sunflower seed sprouts are particularly good, but mung bean or alfalfa sprouts work too)

200g cooked quinoa (115g dried)

Seeds of 1 pomegranate (see Note below)

180g cooked red kidney beans (see page 152)

1 bunch (about 100g) watercress, snipped into smaller pieces using scissors

2 tablespoons shelled hemp seeds and/ or sunflower seeds

Sea salt

FOR THE DRESSING
1 tablespoon tahini (sesame seed paste – preferably not the raw or unroasted kind)

125ml extra virgin olive oil

2 tablespoons lemon juice (about 1 lemon)

2 teaspoons honey or maple syrup

2–3 teaspoons freshly grated peeled ginger

1 tablespoon cider vinegar

Small handful of parsley, leaves only, finely chopped

Small handful of coriander, thickest stalks removed, finely chopped

Mexican rice and black bean salad

This is one for the adults, but you can certainly use some of the components to put together a salad for the little ones too. The physalis (also known as cape gooseberry) is the superhero of the berry world. Closely related to the tomato and native to countries in Latin America, they are a good source of vitamin C, beta-carotene, iron, calcium and trace amounts of B vitamins. Physalis and fruits of the same family, tomatillos and Chinese lanterns, contain 18 kinds of amino acids and all eight essential amino acids. Although red rice is not a typical Mexican ingredient, it adds a lovely texture and flavour to this dish. SERVES 4

For the dressing, combine all the ingredients except the lime zest (reserve for serving) in a glass jar, screw on the lid and shake vigorously until it is well mixed and emulsified.

For the salad, put all the ingredients except the rocket in a mixing bowl and give them a good stir. Mix in the rocket and, just before serving, pour over the dressing to taste. If you have any left over, it will keep well in the fridge for up to a week and is particularly good with mashed avocado and baked potatoes.

To serve, roughly chop the Roasted Spiced Nuts and sprinkle over the salad with the reserved lime zest.

NOTE:
The rice and beans (see page 152 for cooking instructions), the Roasted Spiced Nuts and the dressing can be cooked and prepared at least a couple of days in advance, as long as you keep the rice and beans refrigerated and the nuts in an airtight container. If you choose to use canned beans, bear in mind that they are almost always softer and mushier than cooked dry beans, so consider refrying them before adding to the salad, to add some texture.

⅓–½ quantity of Roasted Spiced Nuts (page 156)

FOR THE DRESSING
Grated zest and juice (1½ tablespoons) of 1 lime

½ tablespoon almond (or peanut) butter

½–1 teaspoon honey, to taste

Large pinch of sea salt

60ml extra virgin olive oil

2 teaspoons finely chopped oregano leaves (or 1 teaspoon dried)

1–2 heaped teaspoons finely chopped jalapeño (about ½–1 chilli), seeds left in

FOR THE SALAD
150g cooked red Camargue rice (65g uncooked)

180g cooked black beans (just tender and not mushy) (60g uncooked, see page 152)

1 red pepper, core and seeds removed, diced

2 handfuls of physalis (cape gooseberries), de-caped and halved

2 celery stalks, thinly sliced on the diagonal

25–50g (1–2 small bunches) coriander, large stalks removed, finely chopped

50–70g rocket leaves

Baked greens

Oat and kale breakfast scones

Always on the look-out for interesting meals to start the day with, I regularly make this for my family and friends. Nutritious, filling and different yet familiar, it ticks all the boxes for a special breakfast dish. Being gluten-free, it is a very crumbly scone, but no less delicious for it. Instead of the kale and nutmeg, you could add lots of finely chopped chives and cayenne pepper, or a little goat's cheese and chopped thyme leaves. Roughly chopped black olives and finely chopped rosemary make a good addition, too. MAKES 9 SMALLISH SCONES

Preheat the oven to 180°C/350°F/Gas 4 and line a medium baking tray with baking parchment.

Heat the olive oil in a pan, add the onion and sweat over a gentle heat until soft and translucent. Add the kale and sauté until tender and cooked, then process in a food processor, or chop very finely by hand, press out any moisture and set aside to cool completely.

Spoon half the oat flakes into the food processor (no need to rinse) and blitz until very fine. Add the rest of the flakes and pulse a few times until the larger flakes are broken down slightly. Add the baking powder, bicarbonate of soda, nutmeg and salt, and pulse to mix.

Add the cubed butter or coconut oil and pulse until the mixture resembles wet sand. Add the cooled kale and onion mixture, the chia seed gel, apple purée and egg, and process until the mixtures comes together. It should be a little on the sticky side.

Using a spatula, scrape the dough out onto the lined baking tray. Form into a square about 2cm thick, then score into 9 smaller squares, leaving them joined together. Bake in the oven for 20–25 minutes until golden, rotating the sheet halfway through cooking.

Carefully slide a spatula under the scones to loosen them from the baking parchment, then separate the pieces using a knife, move them apart a little to give them some room and return to the oven for another 10–12 minutes, to crisp the edges.

Remove from the oven and cool on a wire rack. Serve with butter, hollandaise and poached eggs for breakfast.

A little olive oil

1 small onion, diced

100g kale, stalks removed, roughly chopped

200g oat flakes (certified gluten-free if you are sensitive)

1 teaspoon baking powder

½ teaspoon bicarbonate of soda

½ teaspoon freshly grated nutmeg

Large pinch of sea salt

1 tablespoon chia seeds, mixed with 2 tablespoons water and stirred until a thick gel forms

60g cold butter (or firm coconut oil, hardened in the fridge), cut into small cubes

60ml apple purée or apple sauce (see Introduction on page 143)

1 egg, lightly whisked

Chicory and shallot tarte Tatin

This dish is in honour of a tiny little village restaurant in the heart of Burgundy where I was served something similar but, due to severe language barriers, I never found out more than that they had used fresh orange juice. Braising chicory in orange juice is quite commonplace in both Britain and France and helps mellow the bitterness. Finish with creamy goat's cheese crumbled on top and a drizzle of honey, if serving as a cheese course or dessert. SERVES 4–6

For the pastry, put the flour, salt and mustard powder in a food processor and pulse to mix. Add the butter cubes and pulse to the size of very small peas. Add the egg, thyme and cheese and pulse until the pastry comes together. Scrape the mixture into a bowl and knead gently a few times to form a dough. Alternatively, make the pastry by hand, by rubbing the butter into the flour, salt and mustard mixture with your fingertips until it resembles coarse sand, then adding the rest of the ingredients and briefly kneading until it forms a dough.

Flatten the pastry into a disc on the work surface and roll out, between two large pieces of baking parchment, to a round that will just fit into a 30cm ovenproof frying pan or Tatin dish. Refrigerate for about 1 hour, until thoroughly chilled and firm.

Preheat the oven to 180°C/350°F/Gas 4.

For the topping, melt the butter in the ovenproof frying pan or Tatin dish. Add the chicory, cut sides down, and cook over a moderately high heat for about 5 minutes, until sizzling. Put the halved shallots into any gaps you can find (it doesn't matter if they don't lie flat), cover the pan and bake for 20 minutes.

Turn the chicory cut sides up and season with salt and pepper. There should be some lovely caramelisation and enough room now for the shallots to lie flat between the chicory. Scatter over most of the thyme leaves and pour over the orange juice and bake, uncovered, for a further 10 minutes. The chicory and shallots should be very tender. Turn the chicory and shallots cut side down again and set aside in the pan to cool completely.

Increase the oven temperature to 220°C/425°F/Gas 7.

Remove the pastry from the fridge and allow to warm up for 5 minutes to make it more pliable. Drape it over the cooled vegetables in the pan and bake in the oven for 30–35 minutes, until the pastry is crisp and golden.

Using oven gloves to protect your hands, set a large plate upside down on top of the pan, then carefully invert the tart onto the plate. Leave to cool slightly, then sprinkle over the remaining thyme leaves and cut into wedges. Serve warm with crumbled goat's cheese on top.

FOR THE PASTRY

250g wholemeal spelt flour

Pinch of sea salt

½ teaspoon mustard powder

125g cold butter, cut into small cubes

1 egg, lightly beaten

1 teaspoon dried thyme

30g finely grated Gruyère cheese

FOR THE TOPPING

40g butter

3 heads of chicory (about 500g), halved lengthways

300g echalion (banana) shallots, peeled and halved lengthways

5 thyme sprigs, leaves only

80ml fresh orange juice (about 2 medium oranges)

Sea salt and freshly ground black pepper

Crumbled goat's cheese, to serve

Salmon and samphire tartlets

These posh little quiches are perfect for a special lunch alongside a couple of salads, but also make a good start to an elegant dinner. Substitute the salmon with briefly steamed asparagus pieces if you would like to make a vegetarian version. Or use asparagus if you cannot find samphire (sea beans). This dish really benefits from being baked in deep tart cases, as the shallower versions leave you with too much pastry, too little filling and easily over-cooked fish. MAKES 4 DEEP, 8–9CM

Grease 4 loose-bottomed, 8–9cm tart tins, by dipping a pastry brush in oil and brushing the insides.

Put the butter, flour, chervil and salt in a food processor and blitz until the mixture resembles coarse sand. With the motor running, add the cold water until the dough just starts to come together. Tip out and knead briefly until you have a cohesive, smooth ball of dough.

Roll out the pastry thinly between two sheets of greaseproof paper, then cut out 4 circles large enough to line the tart cases (use a large round pastry cutter or lid of a food container). Carefully press each into a tart tin and refrigerate for about 30 minutes, until firm. Meanwhile, preheat the oven to 180°C/350°F/Gas 4.

Bake the tart cases blind (without the filling or any need for baking beans) for 10–15 minutes and remove from the oven. Use a pastry brush to brush some of the beaten eggs onto any cracks that may have formed in the tart cases during baking and return them to the oven for another couple of minutes before removing and setting aside to cool slightly.

Meanwhile, place the salmon on a small baking tray and bake in the oven for no more than 5 minutes (or less if it is a very thin fillet). Remove and use a fork to gently separate the flesh (that will still be mostly raw) from the skin. Set aside.

Heat the oil, butter or ghee in a small pan and sweat the leek until tender. Allow to cool before using a blender or stick blender to blend it with the eggs and cream (or milk) until smooth. Stir in the lemon zest, juice and mustard.

Divide the samphire and flaked salmon between the pastry cases, pour over the egg-and-leek mixture and bake for 20 minutes, or until set. Allow to cool for a few minutes before serving, topped with a grinding of black pepper and some finely chopped parsley.

FOR THE PASTRY

Oil, for greasing

35g cold butter, cut into small dice

90g wholemeal spelt flour, plus extra for dusting

1 heaped teaspoon dried chervil

Very small pinch of sea salt

1–2 tablespoons ice-cold water

FOR THE FILLING

2 eggs, lightly beaten

1 small salmon fillet (about 130g), preferably wild

A little coconut oil, butter or ghee

1 small leek (about 150g), trimmed, halved lengthways and thinly sliced

3 tablespoons cream, full-cream milk or milk substitute

Grated zest of 1 lemon and 1½ tablespoons juice

1–2 teaspoons wholegrain mustard

25g samphire, roughly chopped

TO SERVE

Freshly ground black pepper

Handful of flat-leaf parsley, leaves finely chopped

Nori amaranth crackers

Amaranth is naturally gluten-free, very nutritious and a protein powerhouse. You should be able to find amaranth flour in healthfood stores, or make your own by blitzing about 1 cup amaranth seeds until pulverised in a high-speed blender or spice grinder. The nori can be substituted for a few tablespoons of chopped coriander, if you prefer. MAKES 40–50

180g amaranth flour

50g ground sunflower seeds (use a mini food processor or a spice grinder and be careful not to over-process)

140g arrowroot powder

70g sesame seeds (ideally black)

2 teaspoons baking powder

1 teaspoon fine sea salt

½ teaspoon freshly cracked black pepper

2 sheets of nori, torn into very little pieces (see Introduction above)

90ml untoasted (virgin) sesame oil, or olive oil

100–125ml water

2 tablespoons tamari or shoyu

Preheat the oven to 180°C/350°F/Gas 4.

In a bowl, whisk together the dry ingredients, including the nori, then pour in the oil, most of the water (reserving a tablespoon or two) and the tamari or shoyu. Mix together, then tip out onto the work surface and knead into a malleable dough, adding more water if it seems too dry, but without letting the dough get sticky.

Divide the dough in half and roll each out to about 3mm between two sheets of baking parchment. Remove the top piece of baking parchment and, using a large, sharp knife, cut each dough sheet into about 20 squares or rectangles. Slide the baking parchment onto baking trays and bake the crackers for 15–20 minutes, or until golden and crispy, rotating the trays once during this time.

Carefully transfer the crackers to a wire rack to cool completely, then break along the cut lines. They keep well for several weeks in an airtight container.

PHOTOGRAPH ON PAGE 51

Watercress oat cakes

The perfect biscuit for salmon pâté or Smoked Mackerel and Watercress Mousse (page 52), these are deliciously crumbly with a hint of fennel and a spicy aftertaste from the watercress. The uncooked dough will keep in the fridge for several days or can be tightly wrapped in clingfilm and frozen. I usually bake one log and freeze the other for later use. MAKES 20–40, DEPENDING ON THE LENGTH OF THE LOGS

100g watercress, leaves and stalks

100g wholemeal spelt flour

200g medium oatmeal (stoneground groats, not oat flakes or pinhead oats)

1 tablespoon fennel seeds, toasted in a dry frying pan until fragrant (be careful not to burn them)

1½ teaspoons baking powder

100g cold, unsalted butter, cubed (or cold coconut oil, cubed)

Sea salt and freshly ground black pepper

Blitz the watercress in a food processor until finely chopped. Add the flour, oatmeal, toasted fennel seeds, a large pinch of salt, a small pinch of pepper and the baking powder, and pulse to mix.

Add the cubed butter or coconut oil and process until the mixture comes together. Tip out onto the work surface and briefly knead. If it is too crumbly, knead in ice-cold water ½ teaspoon at a time, until the dough becomes malleable.

Divide the dough in half and form two rectangular logs (I use the flat side of my large chef's knife to get the sides smooth). Loosely cover with clingfilm and refrigerate for 1 hour, or until completely firm.

Preheat the oven to 180°C/350°F/Gas 4 and line two baking trays with baking parchment.

Remove one log from the fridge and slice into biscuits about 5mm thick. Arrange on the baking trays, leaving some space between each. Repeat with the other log. Bake for 25 minutes, until the cakes are golden and browning around the edges. Leave to cool on the baking trays. They keep well for several weeks, stored in an airtight container.

PHOTOGRAPH ON PAGE 52

Chard and feta savoury muffins

These muffins (not the eggs-Benedict-kind, but the American-baked-goods-kind) are great to take along to a picnic or as an after-school snack. Look for traditionally made, soft cooking chorizo that has no added nasties, and choose the mild version if you are feeding youngsters. If you are vegetarian, leave out the chorizo and fry the onion and chard in a little butter or coconut oil, but add another teaspoon of smoked paprika powder and perhaps a little more cayenne pepper. MAKES 12

Sauté the chorizo in a hot, dry frying pan until the fat starts to render, then add the onion and cook until soft and translucent. Scrape the mixture into a bowl.

Add the chard stalks to the pan with a small pinch of salt. Cook until tender, for 5–10 minutes, depending on size. If they are drying out, add a splash or three of water to the pan. Add the chard leaves and cook for about a minute, or until wilted.

Tip all the chard into a food processor or onto a chopping board, and chop finely. Add this to the chorizo and onion mix, then set aside to cool.

Preheat the oven to 180°C/350°F/Gas 4 and grease a 12-hole muffin tray or 2 smaller cupcake trays.

Whisk the flour, baking powder and spices in a bowl and stir in the parsley.

Whisk the eggs, milk and melted fat in a separate bowl or jug, and pour into the dry ingredients along with the cooled chorizo and chard mixture, and the feta. Using a large spoon, mix only until just combined; do not over mix. Spoon into the greased muffin tins.

Bake in the oven for 25 minutes until golden and a skewer inserted in the centre comes out clean (allowing for patches of melted feta). Allow to cool in the trays for a couple of minutes before turning out onto wire racks to cool completely.

200g traditionally made cooking chorizo (the soft kind), casings removed and broken into small pieces

1 medium onion, finely chopped

300g rainbow or Swiss chard, stalks chopped into small dice, leaves shredded into bite-sized pieces

300g wholemeal spelt flour

1 tablespoon baking powder

1½ teaspoons smoked paprika

½ teaspoon cayenne pepper (omit if using spicy chorizo or cooking for children)

25g (small bunch) parsley, leaves only, finely chopped

3 medium eggs (about 200g total)

150ml whole milk, or milk substitute

50g butter, coconut oil or ghee, melted, plus extra for greasing

200g feta cheese, crumbled

Sea salt

Spring greens and pumpkin seed rye "sourdough"

This is not strictly sourdough, but the long rising time gives the bread a complex, delicious sourdough taste and makes it a lot easier to digest. It seems cumbersome to make, as there are a few steps, but the effort is well worth it, especially if you crave a proper bread but don't have a sourdough starter. You could always double the recipe and make two loaves, slicing and freezing one for later use. Serve with an omelette or a selection of cheeses and chutneys. MAKES 1 SMALL PILLOW LOAF

Steam or sauté the greens in a little water until wilted. Drain and allow to cool, then very finely chop or process in a food processor.

In a large bowl, combine the greens, flour, yeast, salt, and pumpkin and caraway seeds. Add the water and stir until blended. The dough will be shaggy and sticky. Cover the bowl with clingfilm and leave the dough to rest for at least 12 hours, but preferably about 18–20 hours, at warm room temperature. The dough is ready when it feels spongy when pressed with a finger. If you break it open slightly, you will see the threads that have developed.

Scrape the dough out onto a lightly floured work surface. Sprinkle it with a little more flour and fold it over on itself a couple of times. You should not have to get your hands dirty to do this. Cover loosely with the clingfilm and leave to rest for 15 minutes.

Using just enough flour to keep the dough from sticking to the work surface or to your fingers, gently and quickly shape the dough into a ball. Again, you should use enough flour not to get your hands dirty.

Place a large piece of clingfilm or a cotton tea towel on a tray and generously dust with flour. Place the dough on it seam side down, dust with more flour and cover with a second piece of clingfilm or towel. Leave to rise again, 3–4 hours, in a warm place. The dough should more than double in size and the surface should crack.

At least 30 minutes before you are ready to bake the bread, preheat the oven to 230°C/450°F/Gas 8. Choose a lidded, heavy-bottomed (cast iron, enamel, Pyrex or ceramic) pot or dish that will neatly fit the dough (about 20cm) and put the pot (without the lid) in the oven as it heats.

When the dough is ready, carefully remove the hot pot from the oven. Slide your hand under the clingfilm under the dough and carefully turn the dough over into the pot. Be careful not to let dough fold over onto itself. It may look a little messy, but give the pot a shake to evenly distribute the dough.

Cover with the lid and bake for 30 minutes, then lower the oven temperature to 180°C/350°F/Gas 4 and bake for another 70 minutes, until beautifully brown, with a lovely crust. Turn out onto a wire rack and cool completely before cutting. It freezes well in slices and can be toasted from frozen.

300g spring greens, thick core and stalks removed, roughly chopped

450g rye flour, plus extra for dusting

¼ teaspoon fast-action dried yeast

1¼ teaspoons fine sea salt

100g pumpkin seeds

2 teaspoons caraway seeds (optional)

400ml tepid water

Broccoli and beetroot greens pie

Ras-el-hanout is a classic spice mixture used in Moroccan cuisine. The name means "top of the shop", which reflects its expensive ingredients, and good mixtures will contain more than 20 different spices, and up to 100. It is available from most major supermarkets and ethnic grocers, but if you feel up to it, you can easily make it yourself (see page 155). Use chard if you can't find beetroot greens. If you are short of time, you could replace the roasted tomatoes with sliced fresh tomatoes, placed in a single layer on top of the other veg. SERVES 4 (OR 6 AS A STARTER)

For the pastry, put the flour, salt, turmeric and butter in a food processor and pulse until the mixture resembles wet sand. Alternatively, you can do this by hand, by rubbing the butter into the dough with your fingertips. Pulse or stir in the cold water a little at a time until the dough comes together into a ball. Tip the dough onto a work surface and knead briefly until smooth; it shouldn't be sticky or crumbly.

Shape the dough into a flat disc and roll it out to about 3mm between two sheets of baking parchment (the dough sheet can be either round or square-ish). Refrigerate until firm.

For the filling, steam the green beans and broccoli separately until just tender; be careful not to over-cook. Refresh under cold running water and set aside.

Sauté the beetroot stalks in the butter, ghee or coconut oil with a pinch of salt until tender, 5–15 minutes, depending on thickness. Add a splash of water to speed along the process if you like. Add the leaves to the pan and cook until wilted, then tip the contents of the pan into a food processor and leave to cool completely.

Remove the firm dough from the fridge and allow to come to room temperature. Preheat the oven to 180°C/350°F/Gas 4.

Add the sour cream, ras-el-hanout and a little salt to the cooled greens and process together.

Place the pastry, still on the baking parchment, on a large baking tray. Put the green beans in a double layer over the centre of the pastry, leaving a 5–8cm empty border all round. Drizzle the beans with olive oil and balsamic vinegar, and sprinkle with a little salt.

Spread half the Slow-roasted Cherry Tomatoes on top of the beans, then spoon the beetroot greens on top evenly, and top with the rest of the tomatoes. Arrange the broccoli on top and finish with a generous drizzle of oil and sprinkle of salt. Fold the edges of the pastry up and over the filling on all sides, pinching together in places to ensure the pastry doesn't slide down; the filling should still be visible in the centre.

If you are using the egg wash, dip a brush in the beaten egg and lightly brush the pastry with it. Bake for 35 minutes or until the pastry is golden and crunchy. Allow to cool slightly before serving.

FOR THE PASTRY

225g wholemeal flour

Pinch of sea salt

Generous ½ teaspoon ground turmeric

100g cold, unsalted butter, diced

40–60ml ice-cold water

FOR THE FILLING

100g (a good handful) of fine green beans, trimmed

150g tenderstem broccoli (or regular broccoli, cut into smaller pieces)

200g tender beetroot greens, stalks finely chopped, leaves cut into bite-sized pieces

A little butter, ghee or coconut oil

180ml sour cream

1½ teaspoons ras-el-hanout (see page 155 to make your own)

Extra virgin olive oil

Aged balsamic vinegar

200g Slow-roasted Cherry Tomatoes (page 154)

1 egg, lightly beaten, to glaze (optional)

Sea salt

Apple and green cabbage cake

This makes a rather impressive three-tier cake that is deliciously moist, has telltale green flecks and a wonderful flavour. The icing is also good with a bit of double cream whisked into the cream cheese instead of butter. Buy a few pots of organic puréed apple in the baby section of your supermarket, or make your own by cooking down some apples and blitzing into a purée, then freeze what you don't need in ice cube trays. Try to find organic dried apple, as it is chewier than non-organic. SERVES 8–10

Preheat the oven to 180°C/350°F/Gas 4. Grease three 20cm cake tins and line the bases with greaseproof paper.

For the cake, whisk together the flour, almond flour, sugar, bicarbonate of soda and salt in a bowl. In a separate bowl, whisk together the vanilla seeds, apple sauce, eggs and oil.

Pour the wet ingredients into the dry and whisk until just combined. Stir in the cabbage, grated apple and dried apple. Pour the mixture into the prepared tins and bake for 45 minutes or until springy to the touch and the cake pulls away from the sides of the tin.

Leave to cool in the tins for about 10 minutes before turning out and cooling completely on a wire rack.

For the icing, cream the butter with an electric whisk until light and fluffy. Add cream cheese and beat until smooth and well combined, then stir in the maple syrup. Chill in the fridge to set slightly before using to sandwich the cake layers and spread over the finished cake.

FOR THE CAKE

380g wholemeal spelt flour

50g almond flour or ground almonds

280g dark muscovado sugar

1 tablespoon bicarbonate of soda

1 teaspoon sea salt

1 vanilla pod, split lengthways and seeds scraped out

250ml apple sauce or purée (see Introduction above)

4 large or 5 medium eggs

375ml liquid coconut oil (about 300g solid), macadamia nut oil or cooking oil of your choice

300g very finely shredded green (sweet) cabbage, chopped up a few times

2 large cooking apples (about 450g), peeled, cored and finely grated

70g chopped dried apple

FOR THE ICING

200g unsalted butter, at room temperature

400g cream cheese, at room temperature

90ml maple syrup

Choc-mint ice-cream sandwiches

Perfect for hassle-free entertaining, the ice-cream mixture is made a day in advance, leaving only the churning and assembly for the day. The cookies can be made a day ahead, too. The ice cream needs a good 4–6 hours in the freezer after it has been churned, so take this into account when you plan your to-do list. It will seem like a lot of mint to use, but it's correct, and gives an amazing depth of flavour! The ice cream is also fantastic on its own. MAKES 8

For the ice cream, put the chopped mint in a saucepan with the cream and milk and heat until the milk steams – just before it starts to boil. Immediately remove from the heat and leave to cool for 15 minutes. Repeat this step once (or, if you have time, twice) more. Strain the mixture, using the back of a large spoon to press every last drop of minty-ness out of the leaves, then discard them.

Whisk together the eggs and sugar. Add the mint and cream mixture in a thin, steady stream, whisking continuously. Return the mixture to the pan and cook over a low heat, stirring constantly, until it has thickened slightly and coats the back of a wooden spoon. Do not allow to boil or overheat, as the eggs will scramble.

As soon as the custard has thickened, remove from the heat and set the pan in a bowl of cold water (add ice if you have it) to cool. Refrigerate the mixture overnight, then add the chocolate chips and churn in an ice-cream machine according to the manufacturer's instructions. Alternatively, you could freeze it in a large, flat container, removing it every hour to break up the ice crystals with a stick blender or electric whisk. Ideally freeze the ice cream in a flat container that will yield a frozen slab 2–3cm thick, for 4–6 hours, or until firm.

For the cookies, preheat the oven to 180°C/350°F/Gas 4 and line a large baking tray with baking parchment.

In a bowl, whisk together the flour, baking powder, salt and cocoa powder; set aside. Using an electric mixer, cream the butter and sugar together until light and fluffy. Add the egg and mix until blended. Add the dry ingredients and mix until just combined.

Use a tablespoon to drop 16 even-sized amounts of dough onto the prepared baking tray, leaving some space between each. Use the back of the spoon to flatten each cookie, dipping the spoon in a glass of water in between. Bake for 10 minutes, or until set around the edges but still soft in the centre; take care not to over-bake. Remove from the oven and leave on the baking tray for a few minutes before transferring to a wire rack to cool.

To assemble, portion out balls of ice cream with an ice cream scoop, or cut out rounds with a cookie cutter, place on the underside of a cookie and top with another cookie. Eat immediately or freeze until ready to eat.

FOR THE ICE CREAM
200g mint leaves, finely chopped

375ml double cream

375ml full-cream milk or milk substitute

2 large eggs

150g unrefined caster sugar, or slightly less if you prefer it less sweet

90g dark chocolate chips or buttons

FOR THE COOKIES
125g wholemeal spelt flour

½ teaspoon baking powder

Pinch of sea salt

35g cocoa powder, sifted

75g unsalted butter, at room temperature

100g dark muscovado sugar

1 large egg

Sweet potato and nettle coconut loaf

If, like me, you often tear your hair out trying to find the perfect savoury afternoon (or after-school) snack, this one is for you. A snack should be regarded as a mini-meal – a good balance of protein, healthy fats and complex carbohydrates. And, of course, some greens! Don't let the number of eggs put you off as they are partly the reason this is such a nutritious snack or side dish. You can easily substitute the wilted nettle with wilted spinach, as long as you squeeze out the liquid. You could also add a little chilli, cayenne powder or fresh herbs, such as chives, to the batter if you like. Coconut flour is available in healthfood stores and major supermarkets. MAKES ABOUT 10 SLICES

Preheat the oven to 180°C/350°F/Gas 4 and line a small loaf tin with baking parchment.

Bring a pan of water to the boil. Protecting your hands, transfer the nettle tips to the boiling water and blanch very briefly until wilted. Drain and cool (keep the liquid to drink as a herbal infusion, or to feed your plants) then squeeze out all the liquid; you should end up with about 50–55g. Chop very finely.

Beat the eggs with the melted butter or oil, using electric beaters or in a stand mixer, until light and airy. Mix in the chopped nettles, sweet potato, coconut flour, flax, sunflower and nigella seeds, spices and baking powder, with a very larch pinch of salt and some black pepper. Mix until combined.

Transfer the mixture to the prepared loaf tin and top with extra sunflower and nigella seeds. Leave to stand for 10 minutes before baking in the oven for 45–55 minutes, or until golden-brown on top and a skewer inserted in the centre comes out clean, or with a few dry crumbs attached.

Leave to cool in the tin for a few minutes before turning out onto a wire rack to cool completely. Slice when cold, butter generously and serve with a spicy bean dip.

70g nettle tips

8 large or 9 medium eggs, at room temperature

125ml melted butter, ghee or coconut oil

100g coarsely grated sweet potato (no need to peel)

70g coconut flour

25g ground flax seeds or flax meal

35g sunflower seeds, plus a few extra for the top

1 tablespoon nigella (black onion) seeds, plus a few extra for the top

¼ teaspoon ground allspice

½ teaspoon ground ginger

1 teaspoon ground turmeric (or 1 heaped teaspoon freshly grated)

½ teaspoon baking powder

Sea salt and freshly ground black pepper

Honey and thyme buckwheat cookies

These biscuits are very different and, as far as treats go, quite nutritious. Both thyme and honey are highly prized for their antibacterial properties, and manuka honey in particular is used by many to treat burns and cuts. Buckwheat, a fruit seed related to rhubarb and sorrel, is not a true cereal and therefore suitable for people with grain and gluten intolerances. It has numerous health benefits and a delicious, distinct taste. MAKES 20–24

Preheat the oven to 160°C/320°F/Gas 3 and line a large baking tray with baking parchment.

Spread the nuts out on the baking tray and roast for 10–15 minutes, until golden. Remove from the oven and leave to cool.

Meanwhile, beat the butter and sugar together for a couple of minutes, until creamy and lighter than when you started. Add the thyme and honey and beat for another few seconds to combine, before mixing in the egg yolk.

Put the cooled nuts, flour and salt in a food processor and blitz until the mixture resembles very coarse sand, making sure you don't grind the nuts too finely. Carefully fold the flour mixture into butter mixture.

Divide the dough (which will be quite sticky and soft) in half and roll each half out between two large sheets of baking parchment to about a 5mm thickness. Refrigerate the sheets of dough for about 30 minutes, or until completely firm.

Remove one sheet of dough, cut it into cookie-sized rectangles and carefully transfer each cookie to the lined baking tray, using a spatula. Repeat with the second sheet of dough, returning the dough to the fridge to firm up as soon as it gets too sticky to work with.

Bake for about 15 minutes, or until very golden, rotating the tray once during baking. Remove from the oven and transfer to a wire rack to cool completely.

75g shelled, unroasted cashew nuts

75g butter, softened

30g unrefined brown cane sugar

1 scant tablespoon very finely chopped thyme leaves

2 tablespoons honey (ideally thyme honey)

1 egg yolk

100g buckwheat flour

Pinch of sea salt

Courgette and rosemary chocolate brownies

I won't pretend that these are über-healthy, but the courgette adds a delicious fluffiness, and if you resist having the whole lot in one go, they are a wonderful treat. I use dark chocolate, but if your audience prefers the sweeter taste of milk chocolate, use that instead. MAKES 16 MEDIUM SQUARES

Preheat the oven to 180°C/350°F/Gas 4. Grease a square cake or brownie tin, about 20cm, and line with baking parchment.

Cut the courgettes in half lengthways and scrape out the seeds with a spoon. Grate the flesh and set aside in a sieve over a bowl to get rid of excess moisture. You need 200g of grated courgette.

Put the chocolate into a heatproof bowl, sit over a pan of simmering water, making sure the base of the bowl is not touching the water, and leave to melt, stirring occasionally. Alternatively, you can melt it in a microwave. Set aside to cool.

In a large mixing bowl, whisk together the flour, salt, baking powder, cocoa and rosemary.

In a separate bowl, cream together the butter and sugar (it's a good idea to check dark muscovado sugar for any lumps and crush them between thumb and forefinger before creaming). Add the eggs one at a time, beating briefly between each addition.

Briefly beat the milk into the egg mixture, before folding in the dry ingredients, chocolate buttons and walnuts, using a large metal spoon.

Stir in the cooled melted chocolate and then the grated courgette. Do not over-mix; stir just enough to combine. Scrape the mixture into the prepared tin and press it into the corners, smoothing the top.

Bake in the oven for 30–40 minutes (depending on the size of your tin), until a skewer inserted into the centre comes out clean or with a few dry crumbs attached (allowing for patches of melted chocolate).

Leave to cool in the tin for a few minutes before turning out onto a rack wire to cool completely. Cut into squares and keep in an airtight container for up to 5 days.

2–3 medium courgettes

125g butter, softened, plus extra to grease

120g dark (70%) chocolate, broken into pieces

160g wholemeal spelt flour (or half wholemeal and half white)

Pinch of sea salt

2 teaspoons baking powder

25g (about 3 tablespoons) unsweetened cocoa powder, sifted

1½ teaspoons very finely chopped rosemary

125g light or dark muscovado sugar

2 medium eggs

155ml milk of your choice (I use almond)

70g milk chocolate buttons, chips or roughly chopped squares

80g shelled, unroasted walnuts, finely chopped

Raw lemon and lime curd tartlets

This is my version of a popular dessert in the raw food world. I love the refreshing, not-too-sweet taste and the fact that it is supremely satisfying. If you've never sprouted anything before, buckwheat crisps are the perfect introduction to the world of these enzyme-rich and nutrient-dense foods. Raw buckwheat is available from most healthfood stores, sprouts easily and the crisps are a slightly nuttier version of rice crispies, which can be sprinkled on porridge or mixed into granola recipes. You can soak, sprout and dry the buckwheat well in advance, and keep it in an airtight jar. MAKES 6 TARTLETS

Blitz all the ingredients for the crust in a food processor until the mixture resembles coarse, wet sand. Scrape out and press into 6 mini tart tins, 10cm diameter. Refrigerate while you make the filling.

In a powerful blender, blend all the ingredients for the filling until very smooth. If using a regular blender, the result will not be quite as smooth, so you may want to strain the mixture through a sieve. Taste, and if it is too tart, add another tablespoon or two of honey, bearing in mind that the crust is sweet and offsets the filling beautifully.

Spoon the filling into the tart cases and refrigerate for at least 4 hours. Carefully unmould each tart and serve with fresh blueberries and some fresh lime or lemon zest. They keep well in their tins in the fridge for a day or two.

NOTE:
To sprout raw, un-roasted buckwheat (not kasha), soak 2 cups of buckwheat groats in three times their volume of fresh water for 12–18 hours, changing the water (it will go slimy) once during this time. Then drain, rinse off any sliminess, and leave for a day or two in a sprouting jar, mesh bag or sieve, loosely covered with a piece of kitchen paper or cloth, rinsing well and giving a stir twice a day. Once most of the grains have started sprouting (you will see a tiny little tail forming), spread them all out on a tray or baking sheet and dry in a dehydrator or at a very low temperature (about 65°C) in the oven until crisp, usually for 12–24 hours. The low temperature is essential to preserve the enzymes in the sprouts, but if you are pressed for time, you could increase the temperature and reduce the baking time.

FOR THE CRUST
80g sprouted, dried buckwheat
(see Note below)

1½ tablespoons melted coconut oil

125g shelled, unroasted cashew nuts, soaked for a few hours and drained

Grated zest of 1 lemon, plus extra to serve

55g desiccated coconut

Pinch of sea salt

5 large soft Medjool dates, pitted and chopped

FOR THE FILLING
120g shelled, unroasted macadamia or pecan nuts, soaked for a few hours then drained

180ml mixture of lemon and lime juice (about 2 large lemons and 3 limes)

2 large avocados (260–280g each), peeled and pitted

60ml honey

Pinch of sea salt

1 teaspoon good-quality lemon extract or a few drops of lemon oil

2 tablespoons liquid coconut oil

Basic recipes

Cooking legumes

My rough rule of thumb for beans in general is that they will yield 2½ to 3 times the volume (give or take a bit) and twice the weight (give or take a bit) after an overnight soak and cooking. Once rehydrated, beans cook in 15 minutes to 1½ hours, depending on the type of bean. There is much differing opinion on whether to add salt during cooking or after, as some cooks believe it prevents pulses and beans from becoming tender. In my experience this has never happened, and I find a bland bean quite a challenge to eat, so I am in the camp of adding a pinch of salt to the cooking liquid.

150–200g dried beans or lentils

½ teaspoon bicarbonate of soda

1 bay leaf

1 small onion, peeled and quartered

1–2 garlic cloves, bruised and peeled

Pinch of sea salt

5 black peppercorns (optional)

Small strip (about 3 x 5cm) of kombu/kelp (optional)

Soak the beans or lentils in four times the volume of fresh, room-temperature water and the bicarbonate of soda for at least 12 hours, but up to 36 hours.

Change the soaking water once a day if you soak for longer than a 24-hour period.

When ready to cook, rinse the beans under cold running water, then place in a saucepan with plenty of fresh water, the bay leaf, onion, garlic, salt, peppercorns and kombu/kelp, if using.

Bring the water to the boil, then turn down the heat and simmer with the lid on until the beans are tender. If you plan to use the cooking liquid later, you can boil the beans with the lid ajar, or uncovered, for some or all of the cooking time; this will help the liquid reduce and become flavourful.

Cooking time varies according to the type of bean and soaking time (see below), but it will take anything between 15 minutes to 1½ hours. Taste more than one bean to be sure they are tender, as they can cook at unequal rates.

If you do not need the cooking liquid, drain the beans and use them as stated in your recipe.

NOTE:
If you would like to sprout soaked beans or chickpeas before cooking, rinse them and leave them in a sieve, sprouting jar(s) or net for another day or two, or until tiny tails start growing from one end. At this point they are ready to cook.

Cooking time in minutes	Dried legume (1 cup's worth) (after soaking)
10–15	black (or Beluga) lentils, Puy lentils, red lentils, split peas
15–20	green lentils, brown lentils
30–45	aduki beans, whole dried peas
45–60	black-eyed peas, black beans, broad beans, haricot beans, pinto beans, mung beans and kidney beans
60–90	chickpeas, butter (or lima) beans, cannellini beans

Rich tomato sauce

This is one of the most versatile staples in my fridge, and I usually make a big batch and freeze it in smaller portions. It's great on its own as a pizza or pasta sauce, or as a base for a myriad other sauces and soups. MAKES ABOUT 500ML

1kg medium–large vine tomatoes (about 9–11), halved and fibrous stalks removed

1 whole garlic bulb, skin on, cut in half horizontally

2 large red onions (300–350g), peeled and quartered

Olive oil

Aged balsamic vinegar

Pinch of cayenne pepper (optional)

Honey (optional)

Sea salt and freshly ground black pepper

Preheat the oven to 150°C/300°F/Gas 2.

Toss the tomatoes and onions in some olive oil and balsamic vinegar, season with salt and pepper and arrange in a baking tray, cut sides up. Roast for 2–2½ hours.

Rub some olive oil on the cut sides of the garlic, then wrap in foil and add to the oven to roast for at least 1 hour, or until the cloves are soft.

Once roasted, scrape the tomatoes and onions into a blender, squeeze out the soft and squidgy garlic cloves, and blend until smooth. Adjust the seasoning and add the cayenne pepper if you prefer it spicy.

If you're using the sauce as a condiment, add honey to taste

Basic tomato sauce

This has less depth of flavour than the Rich Tomato Sauce and makes a great foundation for many tomato-based dishes. You'll need it for the Spring Greens Lasagne (page 94). MAKES ABOUT 900ML

Butter, or coconut or olive oil, for frying

1 medium onion, diced

Sea salt

2 garlic cloves, finely chopped

2 x 400g cans chopped tomatoes

2 tablespoons tomato purée or concentrate

Large pinch of unrefined brown sugar

1 tablespoon balsamic vinegar

Heat some butter, or coconut or olive oil in a medium saucepan and gently sweat the onion until soft and translucent.

Add the garlic and fry for another minute or so, before adding the rest of the ingredients.

Simmer for 15–25 minutes or until thick and somewhat reduced. If the sauce is too chunky, use a stick blender to blitz for a few seconds.

Slow-roasted cherry tomatoes

Another wonderfully versatile staple that I keep in my fridge. MAKES 425–450G

1kg cherry or baby plum tomatoes, halved

Extra virgin olive oil

Aged balsamic vinegar

Sea salt and freshly ground black pepper

Preheat the oven to 150°C/300°F/Gas 2.

Gently toss the tomato halves in some olive oil and vinegar to coat. Add some salt and pepper, then spread onto a large lipped baking tray, cut side up and in a single layer.

Roast in the oven for 1½–2 hours, depending on how moist you want the tomatoes to be.

Allow to cool before spooning into jars. Cover and store in the fridge for a week or two, or you can freeze them.

Roasted garlic

This makes enough for four servings of Green Celeriac Mash (page 75), but it can easily be frozen or stored in the fridge covered with a layer of olive oil for a couple of weeks. If you find yourself making this regularly, invest in a little ovenproof lidded dish for roasting the garlic.

1 whole garlic bulb

Olive oil

Sea salt and freshly ground black pepper

Preheat the oven to 160°C/320°F/Gas 3.

Without removing the outer peel of the bulb of garlic, slice through it horizontally. Rub both cut halves with olive oil. Sprinkle with salt and pepper, then place the cut sides together, wrap the whole bulb in foil and bake in the oven for 40–50 minutes or until the garlic is soft and squidgy.

Squeeze the flesh out of each clove and use it as stated in your recipe.

Tarragon mayonnaise

This keeps well in the fridge for a week or so and can be enjoyed with almost anything, from boiled eggs and asparagus, to cucumber sandwiches. One of my favourite ways to use mayonnaise is in Mexican street-style corn, where grilled or barbecued corn is slathered in it, then sprinkled with grated cheese, chilli powder and lime juice. MAKES ABOUT 250ML

1 egg yolk, at room temperature

1 tablespoon lemon juice

1 teaspoon Dijon mustard

180–250ml oil (I usually use a mix: walnut, mild-tasting extra virgin olive and cold-pressed sunflower or rapeseed)

10g (a few sprigs) tarragon, leaves only, finely chopped

1 garlic clove, finely chopped

Sea salt

Put the egg yolk, lemon juice and mustard in a bowl with a rubber base or stand the bowl on a wet tea towel to stop it moving around while you whisk.

Start whisking the ingredients with a small balloon whisk while adding the oil drop by drop until the mixture starts to thicken (or emulsify). This may take a while, so don't lose patience and be tempted to start adding the oil more quickly.

Once it has thickened slightly, you can start adding the oil in a very thin, steady stream, whisking continuously.

Continue adding the oil until you have reached the desired consistency. Your mayonnaise should look thick and unctuous.

Season with salt and stir in the tarragon and garlic.

Ras-el-hanout spice mix

If you are unable to find any of the ingredients already ground, feel free to grind them yourself using a spice grinder or a mortar and pestle.

½ teaspoon ground star anise or 1 whole star anise (optional)

Seeds from 4–5 cardamom pods, finely ground

½ teaspoon freshly grated nutmeg

½ teaspoon mustard powder

1 teaspoon ground turmeric

1 teaspoon fine sea salt

1 teaspoon ground ginger

1 teaspoon freshly ground black pepper

½ teaspoon ground cinnamon

½ teaspoon cayenne pepper

¾ teaspoon ground coriander

¼ teaspoon ground cloves

1 teaspoon ground cumin

½ teaspoon ground allspice

½ teaspoon ground fennel seeds

1 teaspoon edible rose buds (optional)

½ teaspoon edible lavender, flowers only (optional)

If using whole star anise, grind in a spice or coffee grinder until powdered.

Combine all the ingredients, mix well and store in an airtight container.

Chinese five-spice powder

Five-spice powder is well known and highly valued across China. It usually contains star anise, cassia (or cinnamon), cloves, fennel, and Sichuan pepper in equal parts. Optionally, ginger, galangal, black cardamom or even liquorice may be added. Ideally the spices should be kept whole and then ground just before usage, so do not make large batches.

1 teaspoon fennel seeds

1 teaspoon Szechuan peppercorns

1 teaspoon ground star anise or 2 whole star anise

1 teaspoon ground cinnamon

1 teaspoon ground cloves

Heat a small, heavy-bottomed frying pan over a medium heat and dry-roast the fennel seeds and Szechuan peppercorns for a couple of minutes, stirring with a wooden spoon or spatula. Set aside to cool.

Once cooled, grind the fennel, Szechuan pepper and star anise (if using whole) in a spice or coffee grinder, or a high-speed blender, until powdered.

Mix with the rest of the ingredients and store in an airtight container for up to a few months.

Horseradish sauce

The root of the horseradish plant (a member of the mustard family) resembles a parsnip and is used in cookery for its sharp, distinctive taste. Once peeled, it can be grated and mixed with other ingredients to make spicy sauces to accompany fish or roast beef. Do be careful when you work with horseradish, as it is much more potent than freshly chopped onions and can sting your eyes if you get too close.
MAKES 160ML

30ml (2 tablespoons) apple cider vinegar

½ teaspoon honey

1 teaspoon Dijon mustard (or if you like it really spicy, hot English mustard)

2–3 tablespoons finely grated fresh or jarred horseradish root

125ml sour cream

Sea salt

Combine the vinegar, salt, honey and mustard in a small bowl. Stir in the grated the horseradish and set aside for 10 minutes to allow the flavours to meld.

Gradually whisk in the sour cream and add salt to taste. Store in an airtight container in the fridge for 2–3 weeks.

Sticky brown rice

SERVES 2

150g short-grain brown rice

280ml water

Large pinch of sea salt

Rinse the rice under cold running water until the water runs clear. Put into a saucepan with the water and salt.

Cover and bring to the boil, then turn the heat down to low and cook gently and undisturbed for 30 minutes, without lifting the lid at all.

After 30 minutes, check all the water has been absorbed by inserting a knife into the centre of the pan and gently pushing aside some of the rice, so you can see the base of the pan. If there's still water, cover again and continue to cook for a few minutes, checking regularly.

Once all the water has been absorbed, add approximately the same volume of water as there is rice, erring on the side of less. Mix the water into the rice well, then bring back to a simmer and turn down to low.

Cover and cook as before for 10–15 minutes, until all the water has been absorbed. Remove from the heat and allow the rice to steam for another 5 minutes, with the lid on.

Roasted spiced nuts

Used in the Mexican Rice and Black Bean Salad (page 127), this recipe makes much more than you need, but you will be glad for it, as it is the most moreish snack you could ever wish for.
MAKES 500G

500g mixed shelled, unroasted nuts (Brazils, pecans, walnuts, almonds, hazelnuts, cashews)

1 egg white, lightly whisked

½–1 tablespoon finely flaked sea salt

2 teaspoons ground cumin

1 teaspoon garlic powder

1 heaped teaspoon ground dried oregano

2 teaspoons sweet paprika

2 teaspoons dried chipotle chilli powder

Preheat the oven to 160°C/320°F/Gas 3 and line a baking tray with baking parchment.

Stir the nuts into the egg white to coat, then add the spices and mix well. Spread out in a single layer on the lined baking tray and bake in the oven for 30 minutes or until crisp and crunchy, giving them a stir halfway through.

Vegan Greek-style "yoghurt"

MAKES ABOUT 200ML

100g young coconut meat without the water

35g shelled, unroasted macadamia nuts, soaked in cold water for 4 hours then drained

1½ tablespoons lemon juice

Pinch of sea salt

1 teaspoon probiotic powder, or the contents of a probiotic capsule

Blend all the ingredients in a high-speed blender, or with a stick blender, until smooth. Store in an airtight container in the fridge for up to 1 week.

Macadamia nut spread

It is hard to imagine something being refreshing and utterly unctuous at the same time, but this dairy-free spread delivers on both those fronts. Serve dollops of it with salads or roasted vegetables, or mix with hummus for a fantastic dip. MAKES ABOUT 250ML

140g shelled, unroasted macadamia nuts, soaked in cold water for a few hours then drained

1½ tablespoons lemon juice

Pinch of salt

½ tablespoon nutritional yeast flakes (optional)

1 teaspoon maple syrup

1 tablespoon olive oil

2–4 tablespoons water, as needed

In the small bowl of a food processor, or using a stick blender, pulse together all the ingredients until the spread has a relatively smooth consistency, with a few crunchy bits.

Resources

Raw and grass-fed dairy products

netherendfarmbutter.co.uk
bartonfarmdairy.co.uk/our-cows
gazegillorganics.co.uk
hookandson.co.uk

Thai young coconuts and raw coconut water

cocoface.com
chilondon.com

Grains, nuts, dried fruit, 'superfoods' etc.

healthysupplies.co.uk
goodnessdirect.co.uk
buywholefoodsonline.co.uk

Grass-fed meat, and preservative-free sausages and bacon

laverstokepark.co.uk
wildbeef.co.uk
peelham.co.uk
eversfieldorganic.co.uk

Index

159

Acknowledgements

I would like to express my deeply felt gratitude to the many people who have been instrumental in making this book possible.

• My fantastic team of recipe testers spread across the globe: Helen Butterworth, Florence Murray, Ida Marie Rasmussen, Vera Cottrell, Marijke Peters, Marianne Brammer, Anneke and Chris Herselman, Melissa Kuzma, Pascaline Monier, Anna Hopwood, Erika Wagner, Catherine and Gary Hoff, Melissa Slomienski, and Caroline Fowler

• My editor, Céline Hughes, for sharing my enthusiasm when I first expressed the idea, and whose attention to detail and calm presence have been equally valuable in seeing it through

• Nassima Rothacker, whose beautiful images will no doubt inspire readers to make every single recipe in this book

• Nikki Ellis, for her artistic guidance and hard work in creating a breathtaking end result

• Food stylist extraordinaire, Aya Nishimura, who steadily churned out dishes AND made them look beautiful

And finally, a HUGE thank you to the three boys in my life who eat the food I serve them with hearty appetites and (almost always) without complaint. You are the reason I go that extra mile.

Publishing Director: Sarah Lavelle
Creative Director: Helen Lewis
Senior Editor: Céline Hughes
Designer: Nicola Ellis
Photographer: Nassima Rothacker
Food Stylist: Aya Nishimura
Prop Stylist: Polly Webb-Wilson
Production: Vincent Smith, Emily Noto

First published in 2016 by
Quadrille Publishing
Pentagon House
52–54 Southwark Street
London SE1 1UN
www.quadrille.co.uk

Quadrille is an imprint of Hardie Grant
www.hardiegrant.com.au

Text © 2016 Zita Steyn
All photography © 2016 Nassima Rothacker
Design and layout © 2016 Quadrille Publishing

Cataloguing in Publication Data: a catalogue record for this book is available from the British Library.

ISBN: 978 184949 716 9

Printed in China